D1442275

EYE ON
Art

FRIDA
KAHLO

by Don Nardo

LUCENT BOOKS
A part of Gale, Cengage Learning

GALE
CENGAGE Learning·

Detroit • New York • San Francisco • New Haven, Conn • Waterville, Maine • London

LIBRARY OF CONGRESS CATALOGING-IN-PUBLICATION DATA

Nardo, Don, 1947–
  Frida Kahlo / by Don Nardo.
    p. cm. -- (Eye on art)
  Summary: "These books provide a historical overview of the development of different types of art and artistic movements; explore the roots and influences of the genre; discuss the pioneers of the art and consider the changes the genre has undergone" -- Provided by publisher.
  Includes bibliographical references and index.
  ISBN 978-1-4205-0850-5 (hardback)
  1. Kahlo, Frida--Juvenile literature. 2. Painters--Mexico--Biography--Juvenile literature. I. Title.
  ND259.K33N37 2012
  759.972--dc23
  [B]
                                                    2012014089

Lucent Books
27500 Drake Rd
Farmington Hills MI 48331

ISBN-13: 978-1-4205-0850-5
ISBN-10: 1-4205-0850-4

Printed in the United States of America
1 2 3 4 5 6 7 16 15 14 13 12

Contents

Foreword

"Art has no other purpose than to brush aside . . . everything that veils reality from us in order to bring us face to face with reality itself."
—French philosopher Henri-Louis Bergson

Some thirty-one thousand years ago, early humans painted strikingly sophisticated images of horses, bison, rhinoceroses, bears, and other animals on the walls of a cave in southern France. The meaning of these elaborate pictures is unknown, although some experts speculate that they held ceremonial significance. Regardless of their intended purpose, the Chauvet-Pont-d'Arc cave paintings represent some of the first known expressions of the artistic impulse.

From the Paleolithic era to the present day, human beings have continued to create works of visual art. Artists have developed painting, drawing, sculpture, engraving, and many other techniques to produce visual representations of landscapes, the human form, religious and historical events, and countless other subjects. The artistic impulse also finds expression in glass, jewelry, and new forms inspired by new technology. Indeed, judging by humanity's prolific artistic output throughout history, one must conclude that the compulsion to produce art is an inherent aspect of being human, and the results are among humanity's greatest cultural achievements: masterpieces such as the architectural marvels of ancient Greece, Michelangelo's perfectly rendered statue of *David*, Vincent van Gogh's visionary painting *Starry Night*, and endless other treasures.

The creative impulse serves many purposes for society. At its most basic level, art is a form of entertainment or the means for a satisfying or pleasant aesthetic experience. But art's true power lies not in its potential to entertain and delight but in its ability to enlighten, to reveal the truth, and by doing so to uplift the human spirit and transform the human race.

One of the primary functions of art has been to serve religion. For most of Western history, for example, artists were paid by the church to produce works with religious themes and subjects. Art was thus a tool to help human beings transcend mundane, secular reality and achieve spiritual enlightenment. One of the best-known, and largest-scale, examples of Christian religious art is the Sistine Chapel in the Vatican in Rome. In 1508 Pope Julius II commissioned Italian Renaissance artist Michelangelo to paint the chapel's vaulted ceiling, an area of 640 square yards (535 sq. m). Michelangelo spent four years on scaffolding, his neck craned, creating a panoramic fresco of some three hundred human figures. His paintings depict Old Testament prophets and heroes, sibyls of Greek mythology, and nine scenes from the Book of Genesis, including the Creation of Adam, the Fall of Adam and Eve from the Garden of Eden, and the Flood. The ceiling of the Sistine Chapel is considered one of the greatest works of Western art and has inspired the awe of countless Christian pilgrims and other religious seekers. As eighteenth-century German poet and author Johann Wolfgang von Goethe wrote, "Until you have seen this Sistine Chapel, you can have no adequate conception of what man is capable of."

In addition to inspiring religious fervor, art can serve as a force for social change. Artists are among the visionaries of any culture. As such, they often perceive injustice and wrongdoing and confront others by reflecting what they see in their work. One classic example of art as social commentary was created in May 1937, during the brutal Spanish civil war. On May 1 Spanish artist Pablo Picasso learned of the recent attack on the small Basque village of Guernica by German airplanes allied with fascist forces led by Francisco Franco. The German pilots had used the village for target practice, a three-hour bombing that killed sixteen hundred civilians. Picasso, living in Paris, channeled his outrage over the massacre into his painting *Guernica*, a black, white, and gray mural that depicts dismembered animals and fractured human figures whose faces are contorted in agonized expressions. Initially, critics and the public condemned the painting as an incoherent hodgepodge, but the work soon came to be seen as a powerful antiwar statement and remains an iconic symbol of the violence and terror that dominated world events during the remainder of the twentieth century.

The impulse to create art—whether painting animals with crude pigments on a cave wall, sculpting a human form from marble, or commemorating human tragedy in a mural—thus serves many purposes. It offers an entertaining diversion, nourishes the imagination and the spirit, decorates and beautifies the world, and chronicles the age. But underlying all these functions is the desire to reveal that which is obscure—to illuminate, clarify, and perhaps ennoble. As Picasso himself stated, "The purpose of art is washing the dust of daily life off our souls."

The Eye on Art series is intended to assist readers in understanding the various roles of art in society. Each volume offers an in-depth exploration of a major artistic movement, medium, figure, or profession. All books in this series are beautifully illustrated with full-color photographs and diagrams. Riveting narrative, clear technical explanation, informative sidebars, fully documented quotes, a bibliography, and a thorough index all provide excellent starting points for research and discussion. With these features, the Eye on Art series is a useful introduction to the world of art—a world that can offer both insight and inspiration.

Introduction

An Unquenchable Thirst for Life

*A*mong many other accolades, Frida Kahlo has been called one of the greatest painters Mexico ever turned out and one of the finest woman painters of all time. Such tributes by art historians, art critics, and art lovers alike developed fairly recently, well after her untimely death at the age of forty-seven in 1954. She did achieve a measure of success in her work while she was still living. But like so many other artists in history, her recognition as a true great in her field did not come until the art world had had a chance to look back on her life and work from the distance of a later era.

In that process of looking back, people were struck at how much Kahlo accomplished considering the tremendous setbacks and disadvantages, both physical and psychological, she had encountered in her highly eventful life. These included bouts of polio and other ailments and the debilitating effects of a bus accident that came within a hair of killing her outright. It became clear that she had triumphed as a painter in spite of these and other disabilities. Yet at the same time she had done so partly *because* of those problems, for she eventually viewed them as challenges to overcome. In the words of the noted physician Valmantas Budrys, who penned an important study of her physical and emotional struggles:

Frida Kahlo is an impressive example of an artist whose entire life and creativity was profoundly influenced by chronic, severe illness; an artist whose talent arose from psychical [mental] and physical suffering yet never was overcome by it. Her work is the best illustration of her life, thoughts, and diseases. We just need to look at them, decipher [them], and admire [her achievement].[1]

An Artist with a Death Wish?

This view—that Kahlo's work was in a sense a window into her life and thoughts—is one of the major theories that attempts to explain the singular nature of the subject matter of her paintings, which has been described variously as dark, unusual, weird,

Without Hope (1945) is one of Kahlo's many works that portrays images of decay and death, which many critics have interpreted as a reflection of the artist's emotional and physical pain.

twisted, creepy, and gloomy. Specific examples include self-portraits that show her crying or that depict her chest opened up and her heart and other internal organs exposed for the world to see. In other paintings she portrayed skulls and skeletons and other traditional symbols of death and decay.

Some art historians and writers have tried to link Kahlo's production of such unorthodox images directly to the several unhappy aspects of her adult life. She was in almost constant pain, they say. Also, she seemed to suffer from acute loneliness and clinical depression, was infatuated with death, and often viewed herself as a social misfit. Some have gone so far as to propose that she was overly preoccupied with death or even that she had a death wish.

The proof often cited for this so-called longing for death consists of a few entries Kahlo made in her diary beginning in February 1954. By that time she was bedridden, taking pain killers constantly, and had recently had her right leg amputated below the knee. Her husband described her as being depressed a lot, and on occasion she also talked about taking her own life. "At moments, I almost lost my reason," she wrote in the diary on February 11. "I keep on wanting to kill myself."[2]

A Reason to Keep Going

Everyone who has researched Kahlo's life would agree that her physical suffering affected her mental condition to at least some degree, and that her mental condition partly shaped her work. That would be only natural for any person stricken with more than his or her share of misfortune. But the consensus of the experts is that this line of reasoning can be taken too far. It would be a mistake, they say, to assume that her frequent preoccupation with images of sadness, illness, and death indicated a deep-seated desire to die.

In fact, some of Kahlo's leading biographers have detected a very different current running through both her personal life and her work. They say that her interest in some of the darker aspects of life was not the result of a death wish, but rather

Opposite page: Kahlo paints at her easel in 1931.

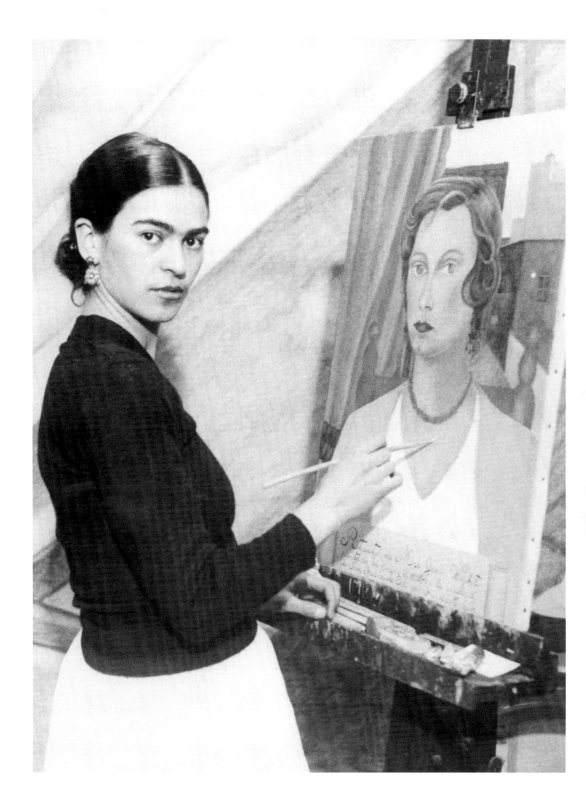

a perfectly healthy way to work through her frustrations and disappointments. Indeed, Kahlo herself always insisted that she was a realist who painted things she was familiar with. These naturally included the realities of her own bouts with injury and poor health. "I never paint dreams or nightmares," she said on one occasion. "I paint my own reality." Another time, she wrote, "I paint whatever passes through my head without any other consideration."[3]

Moreover, despite a handful of very downbeat diary entries, much more of what Kahlo wrote in that journal suggests an ultimately positive, rather than negative, state of mind. As time went on, most of what she wrote and said revealed a firm refusal to be defeated by her problems. On several occasions, in fact, she cited reasons for wanting to live, including her love for her husband and friends and, in return, their love for her. On March 21, 1954, she wrote in a hopeful tone, "I will be able to walk [again]. I will be able to paint." She followed these words with the clearly optimistic statement, "My will is great. My will remains."[4]

Not long after that, on April 27, less than three months before her death, Kahlo made a journal entry that reads, "Thanks to myself and my powerful will to live among those who love me and for all those I love. Long live joy."[5] These words seem to reveal what some observers believe was the real Frida Kahlo, who, in spite of numerous hardships that would have utterly destroyed some people, was desperate to continue to live and love. So she kept on adapting as best as she could to the newest situations she found herself in, which were often very difficult to deal with.

Part of Kahlo's ongoing adaptation to various aspects of her often-changing life was, as some critics have pointed out, her tendency to express herself through her painting. It is true that she frequently painted images having to do with death. But this may have had little or nothing to do with admiring death and wanting to embrace it and more to do with facing the reality of death and in a sense thumbing her nose at it. In this view, as a couple of her biographers have suggested, she painted images of death because she felt it was something she had to do in order to avoid being taken away by it. "I paint because I need to,"[6] she said on more than one occasion, implying that she needed to do so in order to keep on living.

In fulfilling that need on a regular basis—through painting—Kahlo gave herself another, and then another, and then still another reason to keep going, no matter how bad things in her life became. As her biographer Salomon Grimberg put it,

> In reaction to a lifelong sense of inadequacy, of not fitting in [the mold of the average so-called happy person], Kahlo invented and reinvented herself. . . . She created a timeless persona [character] that was mirrored in her art—a sorrowful heroine whose obsession with death provided her with an unquenchable thirst for life.[7]

1

Her Childhood in the Blue House

Three years before Frida Kahlo was born, her father, Guillermo Kahlo, built the Casa Azul, the "Blue House," in Coyoacán, then a pleasant little suburb of Mexico City. The word *Blue* in its name came from the deep-blue hue of the paint that eventually coated its exterior. The structure was U-shaped, and the inside of the U consisted of a lovely courtyard filled with subtropical plants and flowers. That charming family home was destined to be the central focal point of Frida Kahlo's short but significant life. Within its walls, she was born, grew up, dwelled with her husband, and finally died.

Of these key events, the birth took place on July 6, 1907. In her diary, the grown-up Frida later supplied some of the details, along with some vital information about some of her principal family members:

> I was born in the room on the corner of Londres Street and Allende in Coyoacán [at] one o'clock in the morning. My paternal grandparents [were] Hungarian, born in Arat, Hungary. After their marriage they went to live in Germany, where some of their children were born, among them my father, in Baden Baden, Germany—

Guillermo Kahlo. . . . He emigrated to Mexico in the 19th century. He settled here for the rest of his life. He married a Mexican girl, [and when she] died very young, he married my mother, Matilde Calderón y Gonzalez. [She was] one of twelve children of my grandfather Antonio Calderón, from Morelia. [He was from] a Mexican of Indian race from Michoacán and my grandmother, Isabel Gonzalez y Gonzalez, [was the] daughter of a Spanish general who died leaving her and her little sister, Cristina, in the convent of the Biscayne nuns. [Eventually] she left [that place] to marry my grandfather, a photographer by profession.[8]

The Casa Azul, or "Blue House," is the home in Coyoacán, Mexico, where Kahlo was born and lived most of her life. It is now a museum.

Father's Favorite

Frida's father Guillermo also became a photographer. Until 1910 he did frequent work for the Mexican government, including the creation of a photographic tribute to Mexico's architectural heritage. Of the four daughters Guillermo had with Matilde Calderón—Adriana, Cristina, Matilde, and Frida—Frida was always his favorite. "Frida is the most intelligent of my daughters," he said on more than one occasion. "She is the most like me."[9] The father and daughter often spent time together, as he took her with him sometimes when he was out taking pictures of the countryside.

Guillermo was also an amateur painter who used mainly watercolors but also oils. Sometimes while he was painting landscapes in fields or beside rivers Frida gathered pretty pebbles and insects, which she later learned more about by looking them up in books. But other times she closely watched him apply paint

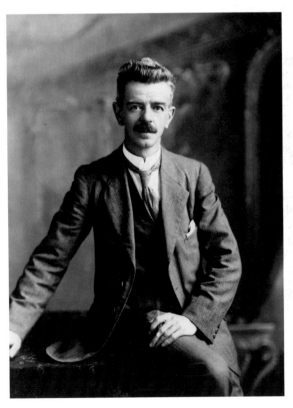

Guillermo Kahlo was an amateur painter who taught Frida, his favorite daughter, to paint when she was a child.

to canvas, noting with a sense of wonder how his brush seemed to become an extension of his hand and arm. She was delighted when he taught her how to use a brush so that she could help him retouch his photos after they had been developed. Years later, Frida would apply this training in creating minute details in her own paintings.

As an adult, Frida looked back fondly on her special times with her father, also recalling that he, like she, had to deal with serious illness on a regular basis. Guillermo suffered from epilepsy, a condition that causes seizures. Frida called his ailment vertigo, or dizziness, because he would sometimes fall down. She recalled: "My childhood was wonderful, even though my father was a sick man. (He suffered from vertigo every

SIGHTS AND SMELLS OF WAR

In her diary, Kahlo recalled some of her and her family's experiences with soldiers from various factions during the Mexican Revolution.

The bullets just screeched past [me back] then, in 1914. I can still hear their extraordinary sound. They used to praise [Emiliano] Zapata in the Coyoacán marketplace with songs. . . . On Fridays they cost 1 cent and [my sister] Cristi and I would sing them hiding in a big wardrobe that smelled of walnut. Meanwhile, my mother and father watched over us so that we wouldn't fall into the hands of the [soldiers]. I remember a wounded Carrancista [follower of Venustiano Carranza] running toward his stronghold by the river in Coyoacán. [I also remember a] Zapatista [who had been] wounded in one leg by a bullet.

Frida Kahlo. *The Diary of Frida Kahlo: An Intimate Self-Portrait*. New York: Harry N. Abrams, 2005, p. 283.

Zapata, seated center, a leader of the Mexican Revolution, poses with his troops.

month and a half.) He was the best example for me of tenderness and workmanship."[10]

Young Frida was not nearly as close with her mother as she was with her father. In part this was because the girl viewed Matilde Calderón as cruel and bigoted. The charge of cruelty stemmed from an incident in which Matilde, ignoring pleas for mercy from her daughters, drowned a litter of baby rats she had found on the property. As for the bigotry, Frida later described how her mother was so devout about her Roman Catholic faith that she viewed all non-Catholics as inferiors. In contrast, from an early age Frida saw all people as potentially equal and good and was disturbed by all forms of prejudice and intolerance.

Prejudice aside, one thing that everyone in the family could agree on was that Mexicans should not be killing other Mexicans. So when the Mexican Revolution erupted in 1910, when Frida was three, everyone in the house was upset and worried about the immediate future. At the time, Mexico's government was headed by Porfirio Díaz, a dictator who regularly used force to stay in power. Various political groups formed to oppose his rule, and a series of battles and violent changes in national leadership raged on and off for roughly a decade in what became more of an extended civil war than a true revolution. In one of the fiercest of the battles, in 1914 the forces of a popular patriot named Emiliano Zapata drove the leader then in charge—Venustiano Carranza—out of Mexico City in a veritable hail of bullets. Frida, then six, and her sisters actually witnessed some of the fighting and helped their parents tend to some of the wounded soldiers. Frida later wrote:

> I saw with my own eyes the clash between Zapata's peasants and the forces of Carranza. My position was very clear. My mother opened the balconies on Allende Street, getting the wounded and hungry and to allow the Zapatistas [Zapata's followers] to jump over the balconies of my house into the "drawing room." She tended their wounds and fed them corn gorditas [a cornmeal cake stuffed with cheese, meat, or other fillings], the

only food available at that time in Coyoacán. [Doing our best to help] were [the] four sisters—Matita, Adri, me (Frida), and Cristi, the chubby midget.[11]

The Imaginary Girl

At age six, Frida experienced another important milestone in her life when she came down with a case of polio, a disease that paralyzes the limbs. At that time the discovery of the vaccine for polio was still decades away and the malady struck millions of people across the world each and every year. Though not permanently crippled, as often happened to children stricken by the disease, the young girl was confined to her bed for nine months. "They washed my little leg in a small tub with walnut water and small hot towels,"[12] she later recalled.

Fortunately for Frida, she was able to walk again. However, the affected leg, her right, thereafter remained thinner than the other. To conceal this fact, she tried wearing multiple pairs of socks and a shoe with a small lift added to the heel. Still, she was subject to teasing and taunts by her schoolmates. One of them later remembered, with considerable regret, "We were quite cruel about her leg. When she was riding her bicycle, we would yell at her: *'Frida, pata de palo!'* [Frida, peg leg!] and she would respond furiously with lots of curses."[13]

Meanwhile, Frida's condition improved steadily because she and her father took her doctor's advice to exercise her legs as much as possible. Under Guillermo's watchful eye, Frida played soccer on a regular basis, learned to wrestle, and became an excellent swimmer. She also climbed trees in the neighborhood and, accompanied by her father, rowed a boat on a small lake in one of Mexico City's parks.

What no one involved knew at the time, including Frida herself, was that recovering from her ailment was not simply a matter of getting proper exercise. Years later it became clear that she had been emotionally wounded by her ordeal. Moreover, the trauma brought on by the polio was very likely worsened

by a debilitating condition she had been born with—spina bifida, a malformation of parts of her spine. "That polio was the only cause of Frida Kahlo's leg and toe deformity is doubtful," Dr. Valmantas Budrys explains. "More likely, the [polio] only heightened an already existing slight congenital leg defect that became more notable as the child grew up, so her right leg problems were probably due to the combined effect of both conditions."[14]

CHEERING HERSELF UP

Kahlo credited her imaginary friend with cheering her up when she was feeling sad or lonely, but in reality she had found a way to cheer *herself* up. She later recalled:

[My imaginary friend] laughed a lot. Without sounds. She was agile and she danced as if she weighed nothing at all. I followed her in all her movements and while she danced, I told her my secret problems. . . . When I returned [to the real world], I ran with my secret and my joy to the farthest corner of the patio of my house, and always in the same place, under a cedar tree, I cried out and laughed at being alone with my great happiness.

Quoted in Jack Rummel. *Frida Kahlo: A Spiritual Biography*. New York: Crossroad, 2000, p. 28.

Whatever the causes of her physical and emotional impairments, for a long while Frida frequently withdrew into a world of her own. In the years following her bout with polio, she developed a friendship with an imaginary girl. Many years later she described the experience in her diary, saying:

I must have been 6 years old when I experienced intensely an imaginary friendship with a little girl more or less the same age as me. On the glass window of what at the time was my room . . . I breathed vapor onto one of the first panes. I let out a breath and with a finger drew a "door." Full of great joy and urgency, I went out in my imagination, through this "door." I crossed the whole plain that I saw in front of me until I arrived at a dairy called "Pinzón." I entered the "O" of Pinzón and I went down in great haste into the *interior of the earth*, where my imaginary friend was always waiting for me.[15]

Immediately before this entry in her journal, the adult Frida wrote, "Origin of the Two Fridas." This seems to indicate that her childhood relationship with the imaginary friend was the initial inspiration for one of the most famous paintings she would produce as an adult. Titled *The Two Fridas*, it shows one version of herself sitting beside another version of herself. Each has been physically wounded by the exposure of her heart. All of this strongly suggests that Frida later concluded the imaginary girl was a reflection of herself. In Frida's mind that girl may have been a more fortunate version of herself who had not been physically and emotionally scarred.

An Avid Reader

Fortunately for Frida, her emotional outlook improved markedly in 1922, the year her father enrolled her in Mexico's National Preparatory School. The best high school in the country, it was located in Mexico City, so she was able to live at home in the Blue House while attending. Her mother objected at first, mainly because Frida, then fourteen, would be one of only a few girls in an institution dominated by boys. But in the male-dominated society that prevailed in Mexico in those days, Guillermo was the head of the family. He outvoted his wife, and when Frida passed the entrance exam it became a done deal.

Whatever her parents liked or disliked about the school, the young woman herself enjoyed it immensely. In part, this was because she was an avid reader and truly took pleasure in learning. Also, both her physical appearance and personality were unconventional enough to make her stand out from most of the other students. According to her chief biographer, Hayden Herrera:

At fourteen, Frida was slender and well proportioned—a fragile adolescent who radiated a strange vitality, a mixture of tenderness and willful spunk. She wore her thick black hair with bangs cut straight across her forehead. . . . Full, sensuous lips together with the dimple in her chin, gave her an impetuous, naughty look that was enhanced by shining dark eyes under heavy connecting eyebrows. . . . Her friends found her fascinating. Many of them recall that she always carried a schoolboy's knapsack, amounting to "a little world on her back": texts, notebooks, drawings, butterflies and dried flowers, colors [paints], and books . . . from the library of her father.[16]

Standing out as she did, Frida naturally gravitated toward other unusual and exceptional students. Soon she was a member of the Cachuchas (named for the peaked caps they all wore), a band of seven boys and two girls who became known for mixing hard work and good grades with playing pranks on teachers and students alike. In one celebrated case they ignited a firecracker above the podium at which a particularly boring teacher was lecturing.

Toward the end of her first semester at school, Frida began falling in love with the leader of the Cachuchas—Alejandro Gomez Arias, who was a few years older than she. Handsome, smart, and athletic, he greatly enjoyed taking long walks with her, during which they talked about all manner of things. When they were apart, even for only a couple of days, they kept in touch through letters. One that she sent him on August 10, 1923, reveals the growing depth of their feelings for each other. She wrote:

You don't know how delighted I was that you had confidence in me as if I were a *true friend*, and you spoke to me as you had never spoken to me before, since you tell me with a little irony that *I am so superior* and *I am so far beyond you.* I will see the basis of those lines and not see what others would see in them. . . . And you ask

HEALTH PROBLEMS BEGAN BEFORE BIRTH

In this excerpt from one of his articles about Frida Kahlo, physician Valmantas Budrys argues that some of her neurological problems (disorders of the nervous system) began even before her birth.

She was born [with] a congenital anomaly: spina bifida [in which parts of her spine don't fuse correctly]. Depending on the severity of the fusion defect, spina bifida may be asymptomatic [harmless] or present with different skeletal [and other] disorders of extremities (for example, clubfeet). . . .

What do we know about spina bifida in Frida Kahlo's case? Her biographical essays usually completely ignore her [spinal] malformation or merely mention it in passing. This is nothing unusual. As is often the case in patients with congenital defects, Frida Kahlo preferred to blame her leg problems on some external causes that took place during her life, [including] polio and trauma. Most of her doctors underestimated spina bifida, too. However, it is very likely that almost all of her lifelong spine and leg problems related [in one way or another] to spina bifida.

Valmantas Budrys. "Neurological Deficits in the Life and Works of Frida Kahlo." *European Neurology* vol. 55, no. 1 (2006): p. 5.

my advice, something I would give with all my heart, if the little experience of my [sixteen] years is worth something, but if good intentions are enough for you, not only is my humble advice yours, but all of me is yours. Well, Alex, write to me often and long, the longer the better, and meanwhile receive *all* the love of Frida.[17]

The Bus That Burst

Arias was with Frida on September 17, 1925, when one of the great turning points of her life occurred. The two had just boarded a small wooden bus that would have taken them home to Coyoacán, when the vehicle collided with a much larger trolley car, which pushed it into the front of a building. Arias later recalled that the stricken bus acted as if it was somehow elastic as it twisted in seemingly unnatural ways. He said,

> It bent more and more, but for a time it did not break. It was a bus with long benches on either side. I remember that at one moment my knees touched the knees of the person sitting opposite me. . . . When the bus reached its maximum flexibility, it burst into a thousand pieces, and the train kept moving. It ran over many people.[18]

Fortunately for him, the young man was not one of those the train crushed. Instead, he was thrown under the moving trolley in such a way that he escaped its wheels, so he was unhurt except for minor bruises and scrapes. Instantly he thought of Frida and looked around for her. Seconds later he found her and was taken aback by the sight. "Something strange had happened," he later said.

> Frida was totally nude. The collision had unfastened her clothes. Someone in the bus, probably a house painter, had been carrying a packet of powdered gold. This package broke, and the gold fell all over the bleeding body of Frida. When people saw her, they cried, "*La bailarina, la bailarina!*" With the gold on her red, bloody body, they thought she was a dancer.[19]

Arias's immediate reaction was to get his friend out of the ruined bus and to a more private, protected place. So he picked her up. But then, as he later remembered, he

> noticed with horror that Frida had a piece of iron in her body. A man said, "We have to take it out!" He put

his knee on Frida's body, and said, "Let's take it out." When he pulled it out, Frida screamed so loud that when the ambulance from the Red Cross arrived, her screaming was louder than the siren. . . . The ambulance came and took her to the Red Cross Hospital . . . a few blocks from where the accident took place. Frida's condition was so grave that the doctors did not think they could save her.[20]

Arias later learned that when the bus began to break up, part of a metal railing broke loose and stabbed through Frida's torso. The metal object had badly cracked her pelvis. In addition, her right leg had been fractured in several places and her right foot had been thoroughly crushed.

A Life-Changing Accident

Rescuers rushed the battered and broken Frida Kahlo to Mexico City's Red Cross Hospital, where doctors operated on her immediately. One of her friends later recalled how the physicians "put her back together in sections as if they were making a photomontage."[21] Somehow, to the relief of her family and friends, she did not die. But her injuries were severe and life-changing. She remained in the hospital for a month and then was bedridden at home for another two months.

In December 1925, Frida managed to start walking again, but soon she felt horrible stabbing pains in her back and a new set of doctors discovered what the first ones had missed. Namely, she had several cracked vertebrae. This necessitated a body cast and more months of bed rest. Confined to her room and unable to complete her schooling, she felt as if her youth had suddenly slipped away and she had been forced to grow up and face a painful adult reality.

As it turned out, the bus accident proved to be a pivotal event for Kahlo in more than just the physical sense. Forced to contend with the monotony of weeks and months on her back,

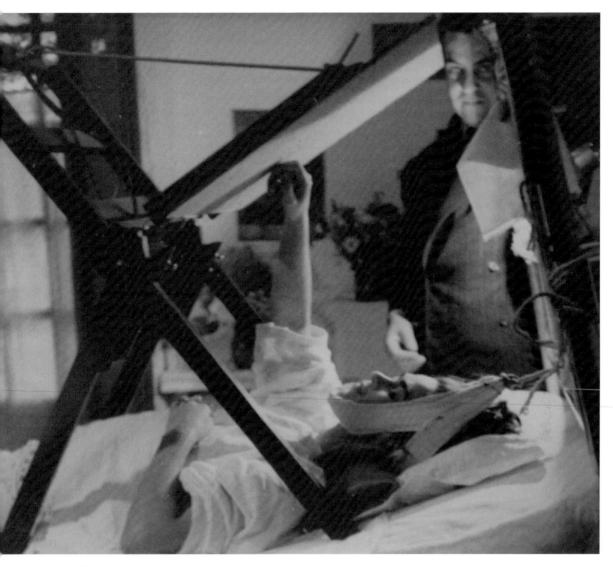

she thought of ways to occupy her time and decided to try paint-ing. Later she told a magazine interviewer:

> I never thought of painting until 1926, when I was in bed on account of [the bus and trolley] accident. I was bored as hell in bed with a plaster cast . . . so I decided to do something. I stole from my father some oil paints, and my mother ordered for me a special easel because I couldn't sit [up], and I started to paint.[22]

Kahlo uses a special easel that allows her to paint while lying in bed. She first used this approach in 1926 to pass the time while recovering from injuries from a bus accident.

One of Kahlo's first paintings was a self-portrait—the first of many. It showed her in a rather formal pose and wearing a red velvet dress with a brocade collar. On the back, she wrote her name, the date, and the words *Heute ist Immer Noch*, German for "today still continues."

Clearly, in spite of the terrible trauma she had endured, she had not been defeated, in part because she had stumbled on a manner of personal expression that gave her two things she badly needed—joy and hope.

Her Two Loves: Art and Diego

I n the moments preceding her horrific bus and trolley accident in 1925, Frida Kahlo was seventeen going on eighteen. Not long after the incident, her family and friends would have agreed that she was eighteen going on forty because dealing with her injuries had forced her to grow up unnaturally quickly. She thoroughly concurred. In a letter to her friend Alejandro Arias, she informed him that because of the accident her life had suddenly changed, and not for the better. "I already know everything" about life "without reading or writing," she told him, a way of saying that she had been transformed into a solemn, serious adult well before she would have liked.

A short while ago, maybe a few days ago, I was a girl walking in a world of colors, of clear and tangible shapes. Everything was mysterious and something was hiding [i.e., there were things about life I had not yet learned]. Guessing its nature was a game to me. If you knew how terrible it is to attain knowledge all of a sudden—like lightning elucidating [lighting up] the earth! Now I live in a painful planet, transparent as ice. It's as if I learned everything at the same time, in a manner of seconds. My girlfriends and my companions slowly became women. I grew up in a few instants and now everything is dull and flat.[23]

Fortunately for Frida Kahlo, this forlorn attitude turned out to be fairly short-lived. In the four to five years that followed the accident, she made two major decisions that ended up shaping the remainder of her life in ways she could not have dreamed before the fact. First, she committed herself to becoming a professional painter. This was a gutsy choice for a young woman who had previously not considered such a move and, more importantly, had never had any art lessons.

The second crucial choice Kahlo made in this period was to become close friends with and marry the noted Mexican muralist (mural-painter) Diego Rivera. Except for the fact that they were united in a wedding ceremony, they were not a conventional couple in any manner. Rather, in several ways they fit the often overly-romanticized image of true soul mates—two people who did not always see eye to eye but who honestly believed that they were fated to be with each other. As one expert observer points out, "To better understand Frida we must also stop and try to understand Diego. He was larger than life, both in personality and in girth, and associated with famous figures in art and politics."[24]

He introduced her to the art world and together they made an unlikely but ultimately unforgettable team almost unique in the history of that specialized world.

Fated to Paint?

Opposite page: Self-Portrait in a Velvet Dress (1926) was the first of many self-portraits that Kahlo painted.

Kahlo began to discard her gloomy post-accident vision of her life as she found that she genuinely enjoyed and even felt emotionally fulfilled by painting. Producing one canvas after another, often while reclining in her recovery bed, she increasingly came to believe that her surviving the trolley accident had not been a matter of mere chance. It had instead been an example of fate intervening.

In fact, a number of her friends, along with many fans who never actually met her, also came to see destiny's hand at work in her life. According to this view, she survived the mishap in order that she might transform herself into a renowned painter who would then bring joy to countless people. The Mexican photographer Lola Alvarez Bravo, who became close to Kahlo over the years, went a step further. She maintained that, in a sense, a part of Frida Kahlo did actually die in the accident and that a second Frida Kahlo was born in its aftermath, a person fated to express herself through painting.

At first, these expressions of her feelings and attitudes were mainly concerned with subjects, especially people, that she knew very well. In addition to her first self-portrait, in 1926, sometimes called *Self-Portrait in a Velvet Dress*, she did portraits of two of her sisters—Adriana in 1927 and Cristina in 1928. She also painted the group of her close friends from school in a canvas titled *Si Adelita or Los Cachuchas* [*If Adelita or the Peaked Caps*] (1927). It shows her boyfriend Alejandro Arias and other members of the group, each accompanied by a symbol of that person's talent or interest. For example, one of the boys, Angel Salas, became a composer, so she painted a sheet of music beside him.

Los Cachuchas was clearly influenced by Cubism, a major early twentieth-century painting style pioneered by the great Spanish artist Pablo Picasso (1881–1973). Cubist works usually consisted of a number of separate, disjointed, compartment-like images juxtaposed together. In this case, the group members and their symbols were seemingly thrown together in a chaotic jumble, although in reality Kahlo carefully placed them where each would be most visually effective.

Los Cachuchas was only one of her early works having a Cubist look, but for Kahlo, Cubism turned out to be little more than a passing phase. Overall as an artist, Kahlo was most influenced by the painters of the Italian Renaissance, particularly Sandro Botticelli (1445–1510). The latter's human figures are rendered fairly realistically and elegantly, but also boldly, with strong lines and often bright colors. These

WHY SO MANY SELF-PORTRAITS?

A large proportion of Frida Kahlo's paintings were self-portraits. Although at first glance this might appear to be a sign of excessive vanity, art experts point out that many famous male artists did multiple self-portraits as well. Noted artist Judy Chicago adds the following historical note.

Dating back to the fifteenth century, women artists asserted their identities as artists through self-portraits, often in an effort to challenge the widespread prejudice that women could not *be* artists. This attitude still prevailed when I was young, when there was no hesitation in saying that one could not be a woman and an artist as well. Thus, it is interesting to note that Kahlo rarely painted herself as an artist, [her] work [*Self-Portrait with the Portrait of Dr. Farill*] being one exception to the rule.

Judy Chicago. *Frida Kahlo: Face to Face*. New York: Prestel, 2010, p. 75.

Self-Portrait with Changuito (small monkey) *(1945) is one of Kahlo's many self-portraits.*

qualities are also seen in most of the faces and figures in Kahlo's paintings. (Such similarities were mainly stylistic, for the subject matter of her paintings was quite different than that of Botticelli's.)

The Lure of Communism

Among the other subjects Frida Kahlo came to depict or express in her early work, either overtly or subtly, were her political beliefs. As an adult, she claimed that back in high school she and some of her friends had become interested in communism. However, a number of historians think this was a bit of romantic musing on her part. They generally believe that she did not begin strongly leaning toward Communist ideals until she began socializing with local popular artists at parties in Mexico City in the late 1920s. In those days, many young adult artists and other sorts of creative people across the Western

A sketch in Kahlo's diary shows names and symbols associated with communism, a political and social system Kahlo claimed she first became interested in while still in high school.

world were drawn to basic Communist ideas. Many wanted to make a statement against social, political, and/or religious tradition. In Mexico, that included the rigidly orthodox Catholic Church and a small clique of rich, snooty landowners who exploited poor workers and held considerable sway in government. Other, less idealistic young artists embraced Communist ideals in order to acquire reputations for being different than the norm and more controversial. Also, at the time communism was new and largely untried as a national political system. Many people who wanted to make their countries better places to live were looking for new ideas and for a while they kept a close eye on what was happening with the then fledgling Communist government in Russia.

The Russian Revolution, which occurred in 1917, eventually resulted in the emergence of a Communist regime headed by Vladimir Lenin (1870–1924). Lenin and his close associates, including Leon Trotsky (1879–1940), promised to give land to the millions of poor, oppressed Russian agricultural peasants and to grant control of Russian industry to the citizenry. These events inspired a number of young progressive people around the world who felt oppressed by local dictators and/or rich land and factory owners.

In Mexico, more specifically, Kahlo and others who early on succumbed to the lure of communism hoped for a Communist takeover in that country. They assumed that such a political revolution would bring about justice, freedom, and equal treatment and opportunities for all citizens, especially the poor and powerless. Like many other Communist sympathizers, however, many of them were later bitterly disillusioned by Russian leader Joseph Stalin (1878–1953). To their horror, he perverted Lenin's and Trotsky's ideas and turned Russia and into a brutal dictatorship, the Soviet Union.

Even then, Kahlo and a few other Mexican Communists held onto their initial ideals, hoping that a fairer, more constructive form of communism might still come to pass in their nation. Today, this seems naive and misguided. But for a young artist in that era it appeared to make sense. As Jack Rummel puts it:

> [To be traditional, conservative] or even middle-of-the-road and [at the same time] be considered an important artist was out of the question. Only a few [Mexican artists of that period] managed to resist this intense form of peer pressure. . . . If one were young and ambitious, it was wise to at least mouth the pieties of social revolution.[25]

One of Kahlo's paintings that captured her early support for basic Communist principles was *The Bus*, completed in 1929. In it, six people are seen sitting inside a fragile wooden bus similar to the one in which she had been severely injured

a few years before. Among the six are a modestly-dressed woman holding a wicker basket, a man dressed in overalls and holding a wrench, and a local Indian woman nursing her baby beneath a colorful shawl. These three passengers are clearly intended to represent the Mexican workers who would, in Kahlo's opinion, benefit from a Communist system. In contrast, the villain of the piece, so to speak, is a "gringo," or white American man, with blue eyes and wearing a vest and bow tie. The gringo holds a bag of coins, symbolizing that he is a capitalist who has become rich by exploiting the workers.

Interestingly, the well-dressed Mexican woman who appears to be the gringo's companion strongly resembles Kahlo herself. This has led some art experts to suggest that she added an element of satire, or spoof, to the painting. That is, she spoofed herself by showing that, despite her Communist ideals, she had sometimes benefited from various elements of capitalism. Indeed, her future husband, the painter Diego Rivera, who also held Communist ideals, was similarly honest and self-critical. More than once he admitted that he had financially benefited from bourgeois (middle-class, materialistic), or traditionally capitalistic, society and government, since members of both had often commissioned his paintings.

The Mystery of How They Met

Perhaps because Kahlo and Rivera and their unique union became in a sense legendary, a number of conflicting stories about how they first met developed over the years. In his autobiography, Rivera claimed,

> One night, as I was painting high on a scaffold . . . there was a loud shouting and pushing against the auditorium door. All of sudden the door flew open, and a girl who seemed to be no more than ten to twelve was propelled inside. She was dressed like any other high school student but her manner immediately set her apart. She had unusual dignity and self-assurance, and there was a strange fire in her eyes. . . . She looked straight up at me. "Would it cause you any annoyance if I watched you at work?" she asked. "No, young lady, I'd be charmed," I said. She sat down and watched me silently, her eyes riveted on every move of my paint brush. . . . The girl stayed about three hours. When she left, she said only, "Good night." A year later I learned that . . . her name was Frida Kahlo. But I had no idea that she would one day be my wife.[26]

A more likely version of how they met was given by Kahlo. "I went, carrying my paintings, to see Diego Rivera," she began.

> At that time [he] was painting the frescos in the corridors of the Ministry of Education. I did not know him except by sight, but I admired him enormously. I was bold enough to call him so that he would come down from the scaffolding to see my paintings and to tell me sincerely whether or not they were worth anything. . . . [I said] "I have come to show you my painting. If you are interested in it, tell me so; if not, likewise, so that

Kahlo poses with Rivera, who was already an acclaimed artist when they met in the late 1920s. They went on to greatly influence each other's work.

I will go work at something else to help my parents." Then he said to me, "Look, in the first place, I am very interested in your painting, above all in this portrait of you, which is the most original. The other three seem to me to be influenced by what you have seen. Go home, paint a painting, and next Sunday I will come and see it and tell you what I think." This he did and he said, "You have talent."[27]

Still another school of thought is that the two first met at one of the artists' parties Kahlo attended in the late 1920s. A story from that period has survived in which at such a gathering she witnessed Rivera whip out a pistol and shoot a phonograph that was playing music he did not like. It sounds like a fable and might well be so. However, he *was* known to do impulsive and outrageous things, particularly when he was drunk, and he and most of the others who attended those parties did quite a lot of drinking.

Forming a Rare Bond

However it was that the two initially met, Kahlo was immediately attracted to Rivera. She was not the first woman to fall for him, as his reputation for womanizing was well deserved. What has puzzled numerous observers from that time until now has been how so many women, among them some beautiful and accomplished ones, found a man of his gross appearance appealing. Rivera was tall, fat, and homely. Also, according to his second wife, he rarely bathed. Yet the available evidence suggests that despite these shortcomings, he had an unusually charming personality that greatly attracted members of the opposite sex.

Other compelling qualities that Rivera possessed were his talent and fame. Born into a middle-class Mexican family in 1886, making him twenty-one years older than Kahlo, he early on showed artistic talent. After taking the best art courses in Mexico, he studied in Europe and lived in Paris's community of first-class artists from 1911 to 1920. Returning to Mexico in 1921, he began accepting commissions from the government to do large-scale murals in public buildings. His paintings frequently promoted socialist concepts and celebrated the native Indian cultures of Mexico. By 1928, when he and Kahlo became

intimate, he was world-famous and widely viewed as Mexico's greatest artist.

In that year, the two quickly formed a bond that was rare for its closeness and the degree to which each trusted the other's opinions about life and especially about art. In fact, each strongly admired the other's paintings and became his or her major and most reliable art critic, as Hayden Herrera explains.

> To her, he was the world's greatest artist, the "architect of life." To him, Frida was "a diamond in the midst of many inferior jewels" and "the best painter of her epoch [era]." Frida became Rivera's most trusted critic. His encouragement of her art was essential to her, and part of her impetus to paint came from her desire to please him. She was, he said, a better artist than he, and he loved to tell of Picasso's reaction to Frida's work. "Look at those eyes," Picasso is said to have written to Rivera, "neither you nor I are capable of anything like it [i.e., depicting human eyes so well]."[28]

The Elephant and the Dove

Kahlo and Rivera were so much in love that they decided to marry and set a date in August 1929. The bride-to-be's mother immediately voiced her disapproval, saying that Rivera was too old and too fat, not to mention that he was an atheist (did not believe in God) and Communist, too. In addition, she pointed out, he had already been married and divorced twice (once to a Russian woman Rivera met in Europe and later to Mexican novelist Lupe Marín). A union between her petite daughter and the huge, uncouth Rivera, Mrs. Kahlo protested with a degree of despair, would be like "the marriage between an elephant and a dove."[29]

Guillermo Kahlo saw it differently, however. To him, the most important thing to consider was that Rivera possessed the financial means to take care of his daughter's medical care, which might well continue to be expensive in the future. One day Guillermo approached Rivera and told him, "My daughter is sick and always will be." To this, the painter replied that he was well aware of the young woman's physical problems. They didn't matter, he said, because he was deeply in love with her. Guillermo then said, "She's intelligent but not pretty," and added "she is a devil," meaning spirited and temperamental. "I know,"

Rivera said, smiling. "Well, I've warned you,"[30] Guillermo concluded and walked away.

The wedding of Frida Kahlo and Diego Rivera took place on August 21, 1929. For the ceremony she wore a dress borrowed from one of her maids, which showed that she was not overly concerned with the material aspects of weddings. The ceremony itself went smoothly. But the reception party that began in the afternoon and went well into the evening was boisterous and rowdy, in part because, as he did at all parties, Rivera drank too much. Kahlo herself later recalled:

> Diego went on a drunken binge. [He] took out his pistol, he broke a man's little finger, and broke other things. Then we had a fight, and I left crying and went home. A few days passed and Diego came to fetch me and took me to [his small house in Mexico City].[31]

One of the first changes that Kahlo's family and friends noticed in her behavior following the wedding was a shift in her everyday attire. More and more she tended to dress in the traditional colorful outfits worn by the women of one of the major local Indian peoples—the Tehuantepec. At first, she wore a Tehuana dress mainly because a friend, Alfa Rios, gave it to her. Seeing his wife in the outfit, Rivera was thrilled because it symbolized Tehuana culture, which had originally been matriarchal, or largely female-dominated. In contrast, Mexican culture was highly patriarchal, or macho—that is, male-dominated. Being a Communist at heart, Rivera felt that there should be more gender equality. So in his view, Kahlo's donning of pre-Hispanic, Tehuana-style outfits was a way for the couple to make a statement against existing Mexican social customs.

As for Kahlo, she wanted to please her husband, as well as to express her own interest in the culture of Native Mexicans. So she started dressing in native garb almost all the time. The characteristic long skirts also nicely hid her thinner right leg, which she saw as a bonus. In addition, these brightly-dyed outfits gave her a sort of exotic quality that turned heads and in time became one of her trademarks.

A Year of Many Portraits

The same year of her marriage to Rivera, Kahlo painted, in addition to her political work *The Bus*, a large number of portraits. These included *Two Women*, showing two Mexican Indian women with strong, attractive features, and several renderings of young native Indian girls, among them *Portrait of a Girl* and *Portrait of Virginia*. Kahlo's early studies of female Mexican Indians were executed at the suggestion of her husband.

He felt that painting members of the native culture would be a show of support for the local Indians, who were sometimes treated with contempt by Mexicans of purely Spanish descent. Another Kahlo portrait of an Indian created that year was *Indian Woman Nude*, showing a topless native woman. Art historians point out that the subject's head is slightly too small for the rest of her body, suggesting that the artist had not yet mastered proper human proportions.

Still other portraits that Kahlo produced in 1929 were *Self-Portrait, Time Flies*, depicting her with a clock visible off to one side and an airplane flying in the sky behind her, and *Portrait of Lupe Marín*. According to noted Frida Kahlo researcher Mike Brooks, Rivera and Marín:

> were married from 1922 through 1927 and had two children together. It seems that the marriage broke apart when Diego began an affair with photographer Tina Modotti. When Frida and Diego married in 1929, Frida befriended Lupe. They went shopping together and Lupe taught Frida how to prepare Diego's favorite dishes. In gratitude for her friendship, Frida painted her portrait. Marín later destroyed the painting in a fit of anger, only to regret it later. A black and white photo of this portrait is all that remains.[32]

Up to this time, Kahlo's paintings had been largely well done, especially for an amateur with no formal art training. But she had not yet developed a characteristic style of her own, one that would allow observers to recognize at a glance that a painting was hers. That changed markedly when, seemingly out of the blue, she produced a canvas showing a man whose legs had been transformed into roots, anchoring him to the ground.

Her Adventures in Gringolandia

The decade following her marriage to Diego Rivera in 1929 was a busy, often turbulent, but generally fruitful one for Frida Kahlo. Her output of paintings was not as large as it would be in later years. This was partly because she devoted so much of her time and energies to maintaining the household and supporting her husband both privately and professionally.

Another reason Kahlo did not sit down to paint as often as she would have liked was that she did a great deal of traveling. In fact, she and Rivera spent much of this period in the United States, where he fulfilled several painting commissions. She jokingly called Mexico's northern neighbor "Gringolandia," a play on the word *gringo*. She made several new friends there, including some she would see or correspond with for the rest of her life. But she always longed for home and was glad when she could interrupt her travels to spend a few weeks or months in her native land.

An Up-and-Down Relationship

Kahlo and her husband spent only a couple of months in his house in Mexico City between the wedding and their leaving for Cuernavaca, a town about fifty miles from the capital. There, over the course of several months, Rivera executed a mural for the local Cortés Palace. It was commissioned by Dwight W. Morrow, the U.S. ambassador to Mexico, as a gift from the United States to the Mexican people. During the months in Mexico City and Cuernavaca, Kahlo proved a devoted and efficient wife to Rivera, making sure their living quarters were clean and that he had good home-cooked meals. While he was working on the mural, she sometimes found some time to work on her own paintings. These included her portrait of Lupe Marín and a self-portrait, completed in 1930, showing the artist wearing a blue dress and sitting in a chair.

However, Kahlo spent much more of her spare time visiting with Rivera on his scaffold at the palace. She often brought him his lunch and/or baskets of fruit to munch on and kept him company while he painted. In the years that followed, their situation was sometimes far less idyllic, and at times even stormy. But inevitably they sooner or later made up and got along with each other again. Hoping to maintain those more upbeat moments for as long as possible, she almost always gave him more attention and personal understanding than he gave her. She knew full well that this was not a perfectly equitable arrangement. But she was willing to accept it

Rivera and Kahlo's marriage was known to have its ups and downs, but even during difficult times, Kahlo remained supportive of her husband and his work.

because of the depth of her feelings for him. One of Rivera's biographers, Bertram D. Wolfe, offered an excellent summary of the unique dynamics of their up-and-down relationship. She often made her needs secondary to his, Wolfe said, because

> otherwise life with Diego would have been impossible. She saw through his subterfuges [deceptions] and fantasies, laughed with and at his adventures, mocked at and enjoyed the color and wonder of his tall tales, forgave him his affairs with other women, his wounding stratagems [tricks, and] his cruelties. . . . Despite quarrels, brutality, [and] deeds of spite . . . in the depths of their beings they continued to give first place to each other. Or rather, to him she came first after his painting, and after his dramatizing of his life as a succession of legends, but to her he occupied first place, even before her art. To his great gifts, she held, great indulgence was in order. In any case, she [said that] that was how he was, and that was how she loved him. [She remarked] "I cannot love him for what he is not."[33]

One of the many examples of Kahlo's showing support for her husband at her own expense occurred when he fell into disfavor with the local Mexican Communists. They were unhappy that he repeatedly took hefty commissions from the government and other groups and individuals in the so-called traditional establishment. They felt that as a committed Communist he should refuse to be what they viewed as a lackey for the social and political forces they despised. When he ignored their criticisms, they finally expelled him from their ranks, and his wife quit the Communist Party to show her loyalty to, and solidarity with, him.

A More Personal Voice

Kahlo sometimes used Rivera, their relationship, and their marriage as subjects for her paintings. An early example was *Frida and Diego Rivera*, finished in 1931, close to two years after their

Luther Burbank

wedding. Hayden Herrera describes its meaning for their relationship, saying:

> Here, Frida adopted the stiff, frontal pose favored by native nineteenth-century [painters] such as José Maria Estrada, whose work influenced Rivera as well. An informative description on a ribbon in the beak of a dove [in the upper-right portion of the painting reads] "Here you see us, me Frieda Kahlo [she sometimes spelled her first name with an added "e"], with my beloved husband Diego Rivera.". . . The painting hints at what the Riveras' marriage would become. As firmly planted as an oak, Rivera looks immense next to his bride. Turning away from her, he brandishes his palette and brushes—he is the great maestro. Frida, whose tiny feet barely touch the ground, cocks her head and reaches toward her monumental mate. She plays the role she liked best: the genius's adoring wife.[34]

This turned out to be one of the last of Kahlo's paintings executed in a standard, generic style. It seemed to Rivera and others who knew her work that she quite suddenly broke out of her more ordinary stylistic shell and found her own, much more personal artistic voice. The transitional painting in question was *Portrait of Luther Burbank*, a work depicting an American horticulturist (plant expert) then famous for creating new kinds of fruits and vegetables. Burbank stands in the center of the painting. As his legs extend downward, they connect with a tree trunk and its roots, which Kahlo showed in a cutaway view of the ground beneath. Directly below those roots, a human body lies, acting as fertilizer for the weird plant/man. "Although it is a portrait of a man," one observer writes, the painting:

Opposite page: Portrait of Luther Burbank (1931) is considered to be the painting that demonstrates Kahlo's transition to a more personal and unique artistic voice.

> is also a dream vision of the subject's life. . . . By contrasting the buried body that fertilizes the plant/man . . . [she] begins to play with the duality of life/death [and] conscious/unconscious. In both cases, Frida seems to be saying, the latter fertilizes the former.[35]

Indeed, from then on the fertilization of, or transfer of nutrients to, living things by either a dead or living body became a recurring theme of Kahlo's paintings. Another fascinating example is *Roots* (painted in 1943), showing the artist lying sideways on and connected to plants in a field. "In this self-portrait," Mike Brooks explains:

> Frida goes back to the theme of nature. She is fusing with a plant, becoming a part of the earth [in] a childless woman's dream of fertility in which her torso opens up like a window that gives birth to a vine. Frida's blood courses through the vine and into red vesicles that extend beyond the vine to feed the parched earth. With her elbow propped on a pillow, she sees herself as a tree of life. In this painting, Frida seems to be nourishing the Mexican earth.[36]

San Francisco and New York City

In spite of breaking new ground in style with *Portrait of Luther Burbank*, in the early 1930s Kahlo focused most of her attention on her husband's paintings rather than her own. Late in 1930 he was invited to the United States to do murals inside the San Francisco Stock Exchange and the California School of Fine Arts (later called the San Francisco Art Institute). While he worked on these paintings, his wife frequently took the opportunity to tour the city and try to get to know some of the locals.

One of the most memorable of Kahlo's new acquaintances was San Francisco physician Leo Eloesser, a specialist in bone surgery. She first consulted him about her right foot, which had remained quite painful ever since it had been crushed in the bus accident some six years before. While examining her, Eloesser found that she had scoliosis, or curvature of the spine, and a disk missing from one of her vertebrae. They became fast

DR. ELOESSER DESCRIBES HIS PORTRAIT

These comments by Dr. Leo Eloesser, penned in 1968, describe the portrait Kahlo did of him back in 1931. At the time he wrote these words, he was about to donate the painting to the University of California Medical School Hospital.

A few notes on the painting might not be amiss. Frida Kahlo de Rivera painted it at my home at 2152 Leavenworth St., during the Riveras' first visit to San Francisco. . . . It is one of her early, early works. Mainly gray and black in tone, it represents me standing alongside a model for a sailing ship. Frida had never seen a sailing ship. She asked Diego about the rigging of the sails, but he would give her no satisfaction. He told her to paint the sails as she thought they would look, which is what she did.

Quoted in Hayden Herrera. *Frida: A Biography of Frida Kahlo.* New York: Harper and Row, 2002, pp. 121–122.

friends and she continued to consult him about medical problems for the rest of her life.

Kahlo was so impressed with Dr. Eloesser that she painted a picture of him early in 1931. Hayden Herrera describes it.

Dressed in a somber suit and a white shirt with an impeccably starched high collar, he stands stiffly, one hand resting on a table upon which his identifying object—a model sailboat . . . is placed. Another identifying object is the drawing signed "D. Rivera" that hangs on the bare wall, for Eloesser was a patron of the arts. The pose is standard for full-length portraits of men

in eighteenth- and nineteenth-century Mexico.[37]

When the San Francisco murals were completed in June 1931, Kahlo and Rivera returned to Mexico. There, he broke ground for a larger, more comfortable residence for himself and his wife. It was actually a sort of a double-house, as it consisted of two separate structures joined together by a walkway on the upper story. The intent was to give each of them enough privacy to work on his or her own art in peace and solitude, while at the same time allowing them to access each other's space when desired via the walkway.

Rivera and Kahlo meet with Anson Conger Goodyear, right, president of the Museum of Modern Art, as they prepare for Rivera's one-man show in New York City in 1931.

Work on the new home had barely begun, however, when in July 1931 another opportunity materialized for Rivera in the United States. The prestigious Museum of Modern Art in New York City wanted to give him a one-man show, only the second granted to an artist in its history. A deal was made for him to display 143 paintings at the show, and he and Kahlo worked almost day and night preparing for the event.

While in New York, Kahlo met many rich, prominent art patrons, representing the cream of American high society. Among those who befriended her and her husband was the immensely wealthy and influential John D. Rockefeller. Kahlo also had the opportunity to observe more ordinary Americans at the height of the Great Depression. She was appalled at the depth of poverty she saw around her, including long lines of people waiting to receive meager handouts of bread and other basic necessities. What disturbed her most was that, while so many people were starving, most of the art lovers who attended the museum to see Rivera's paintings were rolling in money and living comfortable, happy lives. She was unable to understand why such wealthy folk did not distribute the bulk of their fortunes to the poor or to charity, something she knew she would have done if she was in their position.

On to Detroit

The next offer of work Rivera received in the United States came from the Detroit Arts Commission, in Detroit, Michigan. That organization offered him $10,000, a huge sum at the time, to create murals to celebrate the city's thriving auto industry. In April 1932 he and Frida Kahlo arrived and moved into temporary quarters at a leading residential hotel across the street from the Detroit Institute of Arts.

As had happened in New York, the couple found themselves a focus of attention in Detroit's highest social circles. They got to know Henry Ford, the grand old man of the U.S. auto industry, and other major capitalists. Yet Kahlo was not impressed, either by the city's elite or by Detroit itself. In a letter to Dr. Eloesser, she complained:

> This city seems to me like a shabby old village. I don't like it at all, but I am happy because Diego is working very happily here, and he has found a lot of material for his frescos [paintings done on wet plaster] that he will do in the museum. He is enchanted with the factories, the machines, etc., like a child with a new toy. The industrial part of Detroit is really most interesting [but] the rest is, as in all of the United States, ugly and stupid.[38]

Detroit was also where Kahlo painted one of her most important and memorable works—*Henry Ford Hospital* (1932). The painful circumstance leading to her decision to do this very graphic and disturbing canvas was a miscarriage she suffered. She had discovered that she was pregnant shortly after arriving in the city and a local doctor had advised her to rest. But she had ignored him and continued to visit her husband regularly while he was working on his murals. On July 4, 1932, she began bleeding and was rushed to Detroit's Henry Ford Hospital, where the miscarriage occurred. In one researcher's words, the stunning, unsettling painting she did soon afterward portrayed her

Henry Ford Hospital (1932) uses graphic images to reflect Kahlo's physical and emotional pain after suffering a miscarriage.

lying on her back in a hospital bed [right] after [the] miscarriage . . . a large tear falls from her left eye. The bed and its sad inhabitant float in an abstract space circled by six images relating to the miscarriage. . . . The main image is a perfectly formed male fetus, little "Dieguito," [the baby] she had longed to have. . . . The snail, she said, alludes to the slow paced miscarriage. The salmon pink plaster female torso she said

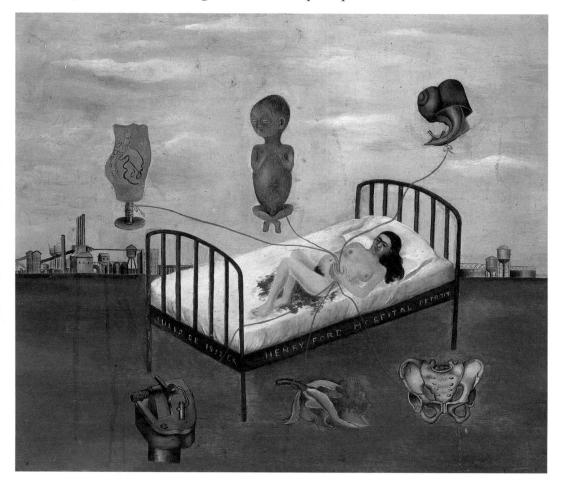

"AMERICANS LACK SENSIBILITY"

Coming from a different culture, Frida Kahlo, quoted here, viewed some aspects of American culture as odd and in some cases even a little disturbing. Particularly bothersome to her was the lack of sympathy and humanity she observed in many members of the U.S. upper classes, who failed to come to the aid of poor, starving people during the height of the Great Depression.

High society here turns me off and I feel a bit of rage against all these rich guys here, since I have seen thousands of people in the most terrible misery without anything to eat and with no place to sleep. That is what has most impressed me here. It is terrifying to see the rich having parties day and night while thousands and thousands of people are dying of hunger. Although I am very interested in all the industrial and mechanical development of the United States, I find that Americans completely lack sensibility and good taste. They live as if in an enormous chicken coop that is dirty and uncomfortable. The houses look like bread ovens and all the comfort that they talk about is a myth. I don't know if I am mistaken, but I'm only telling you what I feel.

Quoted in Hayden Herrera. *Frida: A Biography of Frida Kahlo*. New York: Harper and Row, 2002, pp. 130–131.

was her "idea of explaining the insides of a woman." [As for] the cruel looking machine [in the picture, she had invented it] "to explain the mechanical part of the whole business." Finally, in the lower right corner [of the canvas] is her fractured pelvis, [which] made it impossible [thereafter] for her to have children.[39]

A Series of Masterpieces

This riveting painting revealed Kahlo's artistic talent taking a turn in a new, stark, and artistically brilliant direction. Her husband later summed it up well, saying that from that point on:

> Frida began work on a series of masterpieces which had no precedent in the history of art—paintings which exalted the feminine qualities of [the] endurance of truth, reality, cruelty, and suffering. Never before had a woman put such agonized poetry on canvas as Frida did at this time in Detroit.[40]

The next work in this series of masterpieces, also executed in 1932, was the stunning *My Birth*. Like *Henry Ford Hospital* and a number of her later works, it presents the viewer with profoundly disturbing images of human suffering. A baby is depicted emerging from the womb of a deceased mother whose face is obscured by a sheet. It is clear from the infant's joined eyebrows and other general features that it is intended as a rendering of the artist herself. Behind and above the scene on the bed hangs a portrait of the Virgin Mary, her expression appearing to be one of horror and grief at witnessing the tragedy below her.

When questioned about the painting, Kahlo said her aim was to pay homage to her mother, who had recently died, as well as to memorialize, or honor the memory of, her own recent miscarriage. Besides its obviously disquieting imagery, the painting was noteworthy for its originality. As one expert phrases it, this disturbing depiction of a mother's anguish during childbirth was completely "new in the history of art."[41]

Several Distressing Events

Kahlo and Rivera returned home in December 1933 and moved into the now-completed double-house in Mexico City. In the four years that followed, Kahlo was forced to contend with a string of unexpected and, to one degree or another, troubling or distressing events and circumstances. In the first, in 1934, she discovered that her husband was having an affair with her younger sister Cristina. Not long after this shocking revelation, Kahlo vented her anger by producing one of her most graphic paintings, *A Few Small Nips*. It shows a man standing over the body of a naked woman who is bleeding profusely from dozens of stab wounds he has just inflicted on her. She later admitted that emotionally she felt like the butchered

In 1936 Kahlo completed *My Grandparents, My Parents, and I,* which depicts a young Frida with her parents and both sets of grandparents.

woman, whose open wounds corresponded to Rivera's numerous infidelities.

Compounding the despair and dejection she felt over Rivera's and Cristina's betrayal, Kahlo was in the hospital often in 1934. Once it was to have her appendix removed and she also continued to have serious issues with her right foot, which was more painful than ever. In addition, she suffered another miscarriage. Most of these events were not Rivera's fault, of course. But her resentment over his dalliance with her sister continued to fester until she felt she could no longer live so close to him, and she moved to a small apartment near the center of Mexico City. There, perhaps out of spite, she had an affair of her own, with American sculptor Isamu Noguchi. Even then, however, the strong emotional bond between her and Rivera still simmered beneath the surface and she felt the urge to pay him a few brief visits each week.

Partly because she continued to see her husband, and also because of the tendency for time to help heal old wounds, by early 1936 Kahlo's anger over Rivera and Cristina had dissipated. She forgave her sister and moved back to the double-house. There, Kahlo, who had produced few paintings in 1934 and 1935, completed her now famous work, *My Grandparents, My Parents, and I*. In it, she placed herself at the bottom of a large, colorful family tree. As Salomon Grimberg describes it:

> A gigantic toddler, a nude Frida, stands within the inner courtyard of her home, which is reduced to a miniature playpen. Each end of the pink ribbon she holds in her right hand travels sideways and upward to form a cradle above her head, to hold the image of her parents that she copied from their wedding portrait. On the left, her mother, Matilde Calderón, stares at the viewer, her left arm outstretched gently over the left shoulder of her new husband and Frida's father, Guillermo Kahlo. Growing out of her navel, an umbilical cord is attached to a developing fetus, suggesting she was pregnant at the time of the mar-

riage. As each end of the ribbon arrives at the sky, it splits again in halves. Suspended on a cloud on each side are bust-length portraits of each set of grandparents.[42]

Another important painting from this period was the 1938 work *Self-Portrait with Monkey*. During her painting career, Kahlo produced several paintings depicting her with animals, all of which she kept as pets at one time or another. They included cats, parrots, hummingbirds, Mexican hairless dogs, and monkeys. Among the monkeys, her favorite was a Mexican spider monkey she named Caimito de Guayabal. Some biographers and other observers have pointed out that Kahlo dearly loved these creatures and viewed them as part of her family, perhaps in her own mind replacements for the children she never had. About the 1938 monkey painting and her other works showing monkeys, art historian Frances Borzello writes that they

Self-Portrait with Monkey (1938) is one of several paintings that Kahlo produced depicting her with animals.

> have a variety of messages. In this one, the mistress and her monkey are allied against the viewer. With her head held slightly back, a mature Kahlo looks down on the spectator, presenting herself as a goddess of nature. She wears a strangely primitive necklace of some calcified material and is protected by her little monkey, who puts his paw around her.[43]

ZAPATA'S HORSE

Frida Kahlo and Diego Rivera not only gave each other moral support as fellow artists, but also offered each other advice about both theme and technique relating to their respective paintings. In fact, in one of the more charming incidents from their relationship, Kahlo actually contributed some pivotal brushstrokes to one of Rivera's most famous and splendid murals. Early in 1929, before their wedding, Rivera received a government commission to do a mural in the stairwell of the National Palace in Mexico City. The theme of the huge and impressive work is the history of Mexico, from before the arrival of the Spanish up to the 1920s. In one section of the mural Rivera depicted one of the great figures of the Mexican Revolution, Emiliano Zapata, riding a white horse. Kahlo immediately objected, pointing out that it was common knowledge that Zapata's horse was black. Rivera stubbornly refused to change the animal's color. But when his wife further protested that its legs looked too thick, he smiled, handed her his brush, and urged her to make the proper corrections, which she did.

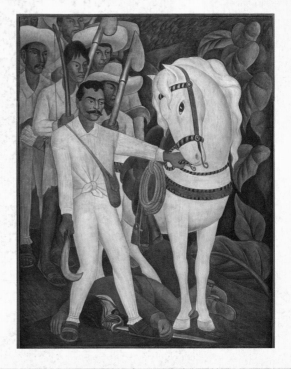

Rivera painted this second image of Zapata and a white horse for New York's Museum of Modern Art not long after he did the first one for Mexico's National Palace.

A Guest in the Blue House

The two years following Kahlo's return to Rivera were also marked by one of the most memorable and important events of both of their already colorful lives. Back in the 1920s, in Russia following Lenin's death in 1924, Lenin's colleague Leon Trotsky had squared off with the thug-like Joseph Stalin for control of the Communist Party and the country. Having eventually won, Stalin had expelled Trotsky from the Soviet Union in 1929. Later, Stalin sent some henchmen to assassinate the fugitive, who fled from one country to another over the years in a desperate attempt to survive. In 1937 Diego Rivera, who had briefly met Trotsky years before, convinced the Mexican government to give the man asylum (political protection). In November of that year, Trotsky and his wife, Natalia, became Rivera's and Kahlo's guests in the Blue House, where Guillermo Kahlo still lived.

Exiled Communist leader Leon Trotsky, holding a cane, arrives in Mexico in 1937 under heavy police guard and accompanied by his wife, Kahlo, and Rivera, left.

During the months that Trotsky stayed in the Blue House, he was heavily guarded day and night by men with automatic weapons. Yet somehow Frida Kahlo, who became fascinated with and drawn to him, found a way to have a secret affair with him, meeting him at her sister Cristina's home. The relationship lasted about a month, and eventually Trotsky and his wife moved out of the Blue House and into a house a few blocks away. Stalin's assassins caught up with and killed him in 1940.

At the time, most people did not know why Trotsky had left the Blue House. But it came out later that he and Rivera had had a falling-out, in part over political differences. It is also possible that Rivera had personal reasons, for late in 1938 he finally found out about the old Russian's brief tryst with Kahlo. Rivera's jealousy over the affair may also have contributed to his request for a divorce from his wife not long afterward. Frida Kahlo would shortly find herself embroiled in still more emotional heartache associated with her husband just as she was at last receiving critical acclaim as a painter.

Her Growing Fame as an Artist

The last fifteen years of Frida Kahlo's life, beginning in 1939 and ending in 1954, were the most crucial in establishing her legacy as a painter. Before this period, few people outside of serious art circles knew who she was. In part this was because she had been standing in the shadow of her world-renowned husband. Finally, she began to sell paintings, to be invited to display her work in major art venues, and to attract the attention of important art critics. Bolstering her image among buyers, critics, and the public alike was the always compelling story of her personal life. On the one hand there was her ongoing, courageous battle against debilitating health problems, and on the other her topsy-turvy relationship with the larger-than-life Diego Rivera.

An Artist in Her Own Right

One of the high points of that relationship was Rivera's genuine admiration for his wife's artistic talent and paintings and his frequent promotion of both in hopes of helping her career. In the summer of 1938, before he had learned about her intimate liaison with Leon Trotsky, he arranged for the famous American film star Edward G. Robinson to come to the double-house and look at some of her paintings. Although he was most famous for his roles as unsavory gangsters, in real life Robinson was a refined, highly educated individual with a growing personal collection of modern art. Thrilled with Kahlo's work, he bought four paintings for $200 each, at the time considered a sizable amount for a little-known artist. This was her first major sale and she was thrilled. "For me it was such a surprise," she later wrote. "I marveled and said, 'This way I am going to be able to be free. I'll be able to travel and do what I want without asking Diego for money.'"[44]

That same year other prominent people in the art world began taking notice of Kahlo's work. Among them was Julien Levy, who owned a successful art gallery in New York City. He requested that she allow him to show thirty of her paintings at the gallery, including the four Robinson had bought. (Robinson generously agreed to loan them to Levy for the showing.) The press release for the show naturally used Kahlo's link to Rivera to help draw customers, yet it also recognized her as being a notable artist in her own right. It read in part:

> An exhibition of paintings by Frida Kahlo (Frida Rivera) opens Tuesday, November 1st, at the Julien Levy Gallery, 15 East 57th St. Frida Kahlo is the wife of Diego Rivera, but in this, her first exhibition, she proves herself a significant and intriguing painter in her own right. . . . In 1926 [it was actually 1925] she was the victim of a serious motor accident (the psychological effects of which may be noted in her subsequent painting). . . . Her paintings combine a native Mexican quality which is naïve [with] an unusual, female frankness and intimacy, and a sophistication which is the Surrealist element.[45]

Kahlo was not happy about being called a Surrealist. The Surrealists, part of a then important ongoing art movement, painted subjects with very offbeat, dream-like qualities that she vehemently denied could be found in her works. "They thought

The Frame (1938) was purchased by the Louvre Museum after Kahlo held a small but highly acclaimed exhibition of her work in Paris, France, in 1939.

I was a Surrealist," she said, "but I wasn't. I never painted dreams. I painted my own reality."[46] Biographer Charles Moffat elaborates, saying:

> She developed a violent dislike for what she called "this bunch of cuckoo lunatic . . . Surrealists." She did not denounce Surrealism, but obviously disliked their ideas about the dream world and psychology [and] didn't like to be compared to them.[47]

Kahlo took the paintings to New York herself in the fall of 1938. About half of them sold, which confirmed to her that she could very likely make a living as an independent artist. While there, she ran into American fashion photographer Nickolas Muray, whom she had briefly met a few years before. The two quickly became close and intimate. Indeed, she regretted having to part with him when she left for France in January 1939. Impressed by her New York showing, French poet André Breton had arranged a similar exhibition for her in Paris. Her paintings were very well received there and one of her self-portraits—*The Frame*—was purchased by the esteemed Louvre Museum, in and of itself a major honor. Also, the great artist Pablo Picasso attended the show and lavished praises on her work. Out of his respect and affection for her, he gave her a beautiful pair of tortoise-shell earrings.

Dealing with Rejection

Upon returning to Mexico in mid-1939, Kahlo moved into the Blue House. It was then that Rivera announced that he wanted a divorce. His exact reasons remain unclear, although a number of their friends thought he might have felt emotionally injured over her affairs with Trotsky and Muray. Although Rivera expected his wife to understand his supposed need to see other women sometimes, he was unable to show her the same sort of consideration.

Kahlo went along with the divorce, which became legal in November 1939, at least to some degree because she was tired of being hurt by Rivera's extramarital affairs, which far outnumbered hers. She later elicited smiles and a few raised eyebrows with her somewhat tongue-in-cheek and memorable remark, "There have been two great accidents in my life. One was the trolley, and the other was Diego. Diego was by far the worst."[48]

Still, it was he who had instigated the divorce and she could not help feeling rebuffed by him. She dealt directly with this sense of rejection late in 1939 by painting what became one of her most famous and recognizable works, *The Two Fridas*. It shows two women sitting in chairs beside each other, each

Kahlo reflects her distress over Rivera's infidelities and the end of her marriage in *Self-Portrait with Cropped Hair* (1940) by portraying herself as masculine and without sexual power.

clearly a rendering of the adult Frida. One is dressed in a traditional Tehuana costume, the other in a white, Victorian-style dress. According to Hayden Herrera:

> At the center of the canvas the two women's hands are joined in a stiff ceremonial clasp. Both Fridas' hearts are extracted [and visible on their chests]—the same

straightforward device to show pain in love she used in [her earlier painting] *Memory*. The unloved Frida's heart is broken. The other Frida's heart is whole. Each woman has one hand in her lap. . . . The Tehuana Frida holds a miniature portrait of Diego [Rivera] as a boy. From its red oval frame springs a vein that travels through both women's hearts and is finally cut off by surgical pincers held in the lap of the rejected Frida. . . . Defiant in their perfect composure, the two Fridas are set against a stormy sky [with] agitated clouds [that] hint at the women's inner turmoil. . . . Frida's world is self-enclosed. Rejected by Diego, she holds her own hand [and] binds herself to herself with a strong red vein. She is her only companion.[49]

In the following year, Kahlo produced two other paintings that were partly inspired by her emotional distress over the divorce, along with lingering resentment over Rivera's affair with Cristina, and his unfaithfulness in general. One was *Self-Portrait with Cropped Hair*. "In this painting," Judy Chicago writes,

Kahlo presents herself wearing an over-size suit and cutting off the long hair that, according to her, was the locus [center] of her control over men, especially Diego. To strip herself of her hair was to lose or give up her sexual power, perhaps as an act of vengeance against him for the unrepentant philandering [cheating] that [contributed] to their divorce.[50]

The other 1940 painting that displayed Kahlo's wounded psyche was quite appropriately titled *The Wounded Table*. Like so many of her other paintings, it featured a version of herself, along with various other people she knew, as well as some symbolic imagery. "The painting resembles a skewed version of [Leonardo da Vinci's] *The Last Supper*, with Frida playing the role of Christ at the center of the table," an expert observer explains.

She is surrounded by an eclectic [diverse] assortment of characters: Cristina's two children, a large papier-mâché Judas, a skeleton, a pre-Columbian sculpture and her pet fawn Granizo. . . . The oversized Judas on Frida's right, dressed in blue overalls, represents Diego who betrayed her [in the] affair with her younger sister Cristina. The figure has his hands on the table as did the Judas that betrayed Christ. This gesture may be symbolizing Luke's words at the Last Supper: ". . . but behold the hand of him that betrays me is with me on the table" (Luke, 22:21). Despite the betrayal, Frida allows the Judas (Diego) to protectively place his arm around her. To her left, the skeleton is holding a strand of Frida's hair, [suggesting that] perhaps she is flirting with death.[51]

Meant to Be Together?

In the months directly following the divorce, Kahlo's health steadily declined. This happened in part because she was depressed over the breakup, but also because of lingering pain from the injuries sustained in the trolley accident and complications with her increasingly sore right foot, which had never healed right. Hoping to dull the pain, she increased her alcohol intake so much that family and friends began to worry.

In addition, some viewed what seemed to them an unhealthy preoccupation with death creeping into her work. Classic symbols of death, including a skeleton, are visible in her 1940 painting *The Dream*, for example. Kahlo is seen asleep in her bed while a skeleton, which has been wired with dynamite or some other explosive, lies in a similar bodily position atop the bed's canopy.

In retrospect, the worries over this imagery were almost surely overblown. First, some modern experts have pointed out, *The Dream* was likely largely meant as a form of cultural expression, as skeletons have long played a major role in Mexican folk

The Dream (1940) is one of Kahlo's many works that depicts symbols of death.

art, especially in the yearly celebration of the Day of the Dead festival. Connected to the Catholic All Saints Day, the celebration remembers and honors deceased relatives and friends. People commonly display pictures of skulls and/or skeletons or dress up in skeleton masks or outfits. Also, Frances Borzello maintains, the imagery in *The Dream* may well have been an expression of the artist's attempt to rise above her constant physical pain.

One of Kahlo's most magical images, this painting expresses the Mexican awareness of death in a way that makes the viewer smile. She dreams so sweetly as her bed floats in space, and when the skeleton explodes, she will die in a beautiful shower of starts and sparks. Far from gloomy, I find it a rare expression in Kahlo's art of her insistence on joy whenever possible—even in the unhappy year [following] her divorce, when this was painted.[52]

Whatever her motivations for painting *The Dream*, Kahlo recognized that she needed help and in September 1940 she visited Dr. Eloesser in San Francisco. He recommended that she get more rest and stop drinking. She followed his advice and as a result started to feel better. Eloesser also urged her to reunite with Rivera. "Diego loves you very much," he said, "and you love him." Regardless of their ups and downs in the past, and those that would no doubt occur in the future, Eloesser told her, she and Rivera were meant to be together. It was obvious to all and as simple as that. "Reflect, dear Frida," he added, "and decide."[53]

Rivera and Kahlo apply for a marriage license in San Francisco, California, after deciding to remarry in December 1940.

In reflecting, as her friend had urged, Kahlo realized that although she was divorced from Rivera, she still felt they shared an incredibly strong emotional connection. This inspired her to begin adding vibrant expressions of love for him in her diary, including:

> Diego, nothing compares to your hands, nothing like the green-gold of your eyes. My body is filled with you for days and days. You are the mirror of the night, the violent flash of lightning, the dampness of the earth. The hollow of your armpits is my shelter. My fingertips touch your blood. All my joy is to feel life spring from . . . the paths of my nerves which are yours.[54]

Rivera could not deny that he still had similar deep-seated feelings of love for Kahlo. So they decided to put aside any past animosities and remarry. The ceremony took place on December 8, 1940, when she was thirty-three and he was fifty-four. Convinced that their relationship would prove healthier if they did not live under the same roof, she stayed in the Blue House and he continued residing in the double-house.

"I Am Broken"

Patching up her differences with Rivera gave Kahlo a major boost that allowed her to concentrate on her painting with a minimum of distractions and emotional upset. During the 1940s she turned out at least forty-nine paintings. Many were self-portraits, including, among others, *Self-Portrait in a Red and Gold Dress* (1941), *Self-Portrait with Loose Hair* (1947), *Diego and I* (1949), and four canvases showing her with her pet monkeys.

Perhaps the most extraordinary of these self-portraits was *The Little Deer*, painted in 1946, another work motivated in large degree by her chronic pain. Although her married life had by now improved markedly, her physical ailments had not. Over the years, the bodily traumas from her accident, illnesses, and failure to take a number of measures that would have given her

Opposite page: Self-Portrait with Monkey (1945) is one of many self-portraits that Kahlo painted in the 1940s that included monkeys and other pets.

at least some relief combined to take an awful toll. In Salomon Grimberg's words:

> The effects of polio had shortened her right leg, and further damage had been done because she never wore an orthopedic shoe or brace. Kahlo chose regular shoes instead and walked about as if the injury could be overlooked. Unfortunately, it could not, and her condition worsened little by little. . . . Later, her spinal column [became] scoliotic. This curvature of the spine [dislocated] several discs, putting pressure on blood vessels and nerve endings. The result [was] diminished blood flow to her right leg, making it more vulnerable to . . . ulcers and the dangerous state that preceded its amputation.[55]

Hoping to end her back pain, Kahlo underwent a major back operation in New York in 1946. When it failed to achieve its goal, she channeled her disappointment and bitterness into the creation of *The Little Deer*. It shows her head and face superimposed on the body of a deer (modeled on her pet deer Granizo), whose body has been pierced by numerous arrows. The doomed creature appeared to be trapped in a clearing in a dense forest, as one observer puts it, "transmitting a feeling of fear and desperation, with no way to escape from the situation."[56] In a similar manner, Frida Kahlo felt trapped in a steadily descending spiral of physical impairment and seemingly unending pain.

In contrast, sometimes she turned such despair around and used her paintings to express her feelings of defiance for the physical problems that tortured her. One of the more striking examples was *The Broken Column* (1944). It shows her encased in one of the corsets a doctor had earlier prescribed to keep her body rigid during the healing process. Her ruined spine is exposed for all to see through a bodily cutaway and her skin is cruelly pierced by numerous nails in a manner reminiscent of traditional depictions of the spikes nailing Jesus Christ to his cross. Art critic Richard Dorment offers a more detailed description:

UNABLE TO SIT UPRIGHT

The Broken Column *(1944) remains one of Frida Kahlo's masterpieces and most stunning and controversial works. Dr. Valmantas Budrys, who has studied Kahlo's life and work in considerable detail, relates the painting to the physical traumas that plagued her.*

One of the most shattering artistic testimonies of the impact of the spinal trauma on her continuous suffering is a self-portrait with a broken column. In 1944, when Frida Kahlo painted this masterpiece, her health had deteriorated to the point where she, unable to sit upright without being tied to the back of a chair, was encased in a steel corset to support her spine. Her spinal column, represented as an ancient pillar broken in several places, plenty of nails sticking into her naked body (note the nails going down the right side of the blanket covering the lower part of her body), and the fissured, dry, bare landscape became a symbol of the artist's pain and solitude. Though very impressive, this famous painting, stressing the broken spinal column as the main source of her excruciating pain and suffering, overestimates the role of the spinal column injury from a neurological point of view. It is noteworthy that medical professionals later also overestimated her injuries, performing numerous unnecessary operations.

Valmantas Budrys. "Neurological Deficits in the Life and Works of Frida Kahlo." *European Neurology* vol. 55, no. 1 (2006): p. 7.

The Broken Column shows Kahlo's nude body rent in two to expose a broken classical column, her spine. Though still a young woman, she shows herself in three-quarter-length format, with hands extended downward and palms open, in the pose of a traditional Man of Sorrows. The two halves of her torso are held together by a brace or corset. Nails pierce her flesh, and tears course down her face. Kahlo's genius lay in her ability to give visual form to physical suffering, and, conversely, to externalize mental anguish by showing it in the form of bodily pain. In the artist Diego Rivera's memorable phrase, her paintings reveal "the biological truth of her feelings."[57]

In spite of the manner in which the painting illustrates graphic pain, it does not depict defeat. Rather, it displays the artist's stoic pride that she is able to withstand whatever torments nature and fate can dish out, to keep on going, and to make the best of an imperfect but praiseworthy life.

"I am not sick," Kahlo insisted on more than one occasion. "I am broken. But I am happy as long as I can paint."[58]

Escape at Last

Fortunately for Frida Kahlo, she *was* able to continue turning out paintings even as her physical problems grew increasingly worse in the early 1950s. Between 1950 and 1954 she did twenty-two canvases, among them a portrait of her father, Guillermo, completed in 1951, ten years after he had passed away. Also in this period she did a number of still lifes, many of them depicting food, especially fruit.

There were in addition two unusual self-portraits. One is titled *Self-Portrait with a Portrait of Diego on the Breast and Maria Between the Eyebrows*. It shows Kahlo as she had looked in her twenties. An image of Rivera, wearing a hat, appears on her chest, the face of noted Mexican actress Maria Felix (one of Rivera's former lovers) is etched onto her forehead, one of Kahlo's pet dogs looms protectively behind her left shoulder, and a Christ-like face adorns the sun's disk in the sky behind her. Contrasting with this hodgepodge of symbolic elements, the other painting, *Self-Portrait with the Portrait of Dr. Farill*,

depicts Kahlo in a wheelchair with a portrait of Juan Farill, one of her Mexico City physicians, resting beside her.

The wheelchair in the picture was neither symbolic nor whimsical. Over time Kahlo's handicapped spine and right leg forced her to use a wheelchair, and eventually she was permanently bedridden. Early in 1953 she learned that she had been

PAINTING HERSELF INTO EXISTENCE?

Noted modern artist Judy Chicago here suggests some psychological meanings inherent in the 1951 canvas Self-Portrait with the Portrait of Dr. Farill. *In this painting, Kahlo is seen sitting in a wheelchair beside her easel, which holds a finished portrait of Farill, one of her more trusted doctors.*

In this work, the doctor stares at Kahlo in a look that is almost more intimate than that of a lover, perhaps because she depended so heavily upon physicians to maintain her steadily deteriorating body. Her palette [as seen in the painting]—which contains no paint—is like a bleeding heart. She clasps it in one hand, as if she can paint herself into existence with the tiny brushes that hover over its surface.

Judy Chicago. *Frida Kahlo: Face to Face*. New York: Prestel, 2010, p. 75.

granted the honor of her first one-woman art show in her native land. When the exhibition opened in April, an ambulance, accompanied by a police escort, carried her to the Mexico City gallery. There, she greeted friends and members of the public alike while lying in her bed, which had been transported from the Blue House. Her friend, Lola Alvarez Bravo, later recalled, "We asked people to keep walking, to greet her and then to concentrate on the exhibition itself. . . . There was really a mob, not only the art world, the critics, and her friends, but quite a lot of unexpected people." Another friend remembered, "It was a little bit like a Surrealist act, with Frida like the Sphinx of the Night, presenting herself in the gallery in her bed. It was all theater."[59]

The show, which all agreed was an enormous success, was Kahlo's last major public appearance. Later that year her right leg became badly infected and doctors had to amputate everything below the knee. Refusing to let this setback destroy her, not long afterward she quipped, "Feet, what do I need you for when I have wings to fly?"[60]

The last time that most of Kahlo's family and friends saw her alive was at a huge birthday party given for her at the Blue House on July 6, 1954. She turned forty-seven that day. As usual, she dressed to the hilt in one of her brilliantly festive Indian costumes and after some men carried her downstairs to the dining room, she was the life of the party. A good many of those in attendance were glad to remember her that way. Despite her long, heroic, passionate fight for life, Frida Kahlo died in her sleep a week later, early in the morning of July 13, 1954.

Her soul mate, Diego Rivera, was in his studio in the double-house when the family chauffeur arrived with the tragic news. A witness later told how the hulking muralist, normally brimming with energy and exuding a vigorous vitality, "became an old man in a few hours."[61] He proceeded to lock himself in his bedroom and for several hours refused to let anyone in. It will never be known whether he found some shred of comfort, as others did, in the realization that at last his wife was beyond pain. Certainly the metaphor from one of her most famous paintings was too obvious to miss. The long-suffering little deer had at last made good her escape from her forest of agony.

Her Legacy
of Optimism

In the hours and days following Frida Kahlo's untimely passing, people all across Mexico wanted to know how she had met her end. The official cause given by her doctors was a pulmonary embolism, a clot that had formed in one of her limbs, traveled through her bloodstream, and lodged in one of her lungs. Some of those close to her also noticed that she had taken several sleeping pills on the evening prior to her death. This fact led a few writers and other observers over the years to theorize that she may have tried to kill herself with the pills. However, the consensus of most experts is that she did not take enough pills to cause her body to completely shut down.

Moreover, Rivera and most others close to Kahlo insisted that she did not want to die, even though she occasionally remarked that her chronic pain was very difficult to live with. Despite her serious ailments, they said, she was full of life. Indeed, she wanted to live as long as possible so that she could be with Rivera and carry on her painting, both of which she was deeply passionate about.

In fact, most available evidence suggests that Kahlo was an optimist at heart. It was an attitude that could be plainly seen in her fervent love of people, family, animals, the arts, parties, and life in general. The same positive outlook survived in the legacy of hope she left behind for artists and others who endure chronic pain and/or other obstacles in their path to achieving success and happiness. As Carlos Fuentes, one of Mexico's leading novelists, puts it:

> Frida found a way of painting pain, of permitting us to see pain and in so doing, reflecting the pain of the world. . . . She is a figure that represents the conquest of adversity, that represents how, against hell and high water, a person is able to . . . reinvent themselves and make [his or her] life be personally fulfilling. . . . Frida Kahlo in that sense is a symbol of hope, of power, of empowerment, for a variety of sectors of our population who are undergoing adverse conditions.[62]

Back in the Blue House

That legacy of hope began to emerge almost immediately after Kahlo's death and the series of events that comprised her funeral service. During the afternoon of the day she passed, a few of her female friends braided her hair and put on some of her jewelry. After she had been placed in a plain, gray, wooden coffin, they put a bouquet of flowers behind her head. Next the coffin was removed from the Blue House and taken to the Palace of Fine Arts, the country's most imposing and esteemed cultural center. There, Kahlo's body, visible in the open coffin, remained throughout the evening and early morning of the following day, as many hundreds of people came to pay their respects.

Later in the morning of July 14, 1954, an honor guard, including Rivera and former Mexican president Lázaro Cardenas, carried the coffin outside to a waiting hearse. Then they and more than five hundred others, some of them weeping openly, solemnly followed the hearse down the street to the crematorium. While Rivera, Cardenas, and a number of others watched, the body was burned to ashes. When the cremation

was complete, Rivera gathered his wife's ashes, placed them in a cedar box, and took them home.

The following year, Rivera donated the Blue House to the Mexican people under the condition that it should become a museum dedicated to Frida Kahlo. When that institution formally opened in 1958, her ashes, now in a sack, were in plain view on her bed. (Some of her relatives and friends were happy to see that she was back in the Blue House, where they, like she, felt she belonged.) Most of the other items in the house remained as they had been when she left home for the last time in her coffin. Many of those who have visited the place since that time have commented that it wonderfully reflects and preserves her singular persona. Indeed, they leave the house feeling that somehow they knew her. Hayden Herrera points out that this is because:

> The relics displayed there—Frida's costumes, jewelry, toys, dolls, letters, books, art materials, her love notes to Diego, her marvelous collection of popular art—offer a vivid picture of her personality and of the ambience [atmosphere] in which she lived and worked. They create the perfect setting for those of her paintings and drawings that hang in what was once her living room. Upstairs, in Frida's studio, her wheelchair is drawn up before her easel. . . . The museum does more than create an atmosphere. It serves to convince us of

Kahlo's studio at the Blue House, which is now a museum, includes her paints and easels as well as the wheelchair she sat in while she worked.

HER SOUL MOVING THROUGH TIME

Over the years, many people have wondered or asked why Frida Kahlo painted so many self-portraits. One of Mexico's finest modern writers, Carlos Fuentes, answered this question in the following manner.

Because she is a woman who cannot reveal the pain inside her except through the painting of her own self. If you look inside yourself, I forgot who said this, I think it was [a] Greek philosopher [who] said, "If you could see yourself inside yourself, you would die of fear of what you saw." Well, she saw. She saw what was inside herself, and she painted it.

This is more than mirror images of Frida Kahlo; these are portraits of her soul. I think that it's Rembrandt who painted his soul, [and] Van Gogh [also] painted his soul. It is not simply a photograph or a mirror image of the painter. . . . When you see Rembrandt going from youth to old age in self-portraits, it is marvelous the way he understood his soul as it aged. It is not only a picture of a man . . . whose hair is going white and who has wrinkles. It is Rembrandt's soul moving through time. And this is also what Frida Kahlo did. It is a painting of her soul more than of her figure.

Interview with Carlos Fuentes by Amy Stechler, 2005. *The Life and Times of Frida Kahlo*: PBS. www.pbs.org /weta/fridakahlo/today/fuentes.html.

the specificity and realism of the fantastic imagery in Frida's paintings and of the intimate bond between her life and her art.[63]

Diego Rivera did not live long enough to see the museum's official opening. He died at the age of seventy of a heart attack in his studio in the double-house on November 24, 1957. He had wanted his ashes to be mixed with Kahlo's. But those who took charge of his body refused to honor that request and instead laid his remains to rest in Mexico City's Rotonda de los Hombres Ilustres (Rotunda of Illustrious Persons).

A Cult Figure

When Rivera died, he was widely seen as Mexico's finest painter and enjoyed worldwide recognition as an artist. In contrast, when Kahlo passed away three years before, she was familiar to the members of most artistic circles but still little known to the general public in the United Sates and most other Western countries. The main reason was that she and her work had been overshadowed by her husband and his renowned murals.

Kahlo's near obscurity lasted a couple more decades, but then rapidly began to change. As has been the case with many other gifted artists over the centuries, she became far more popular and celebrated well after her death than she had been in life. Knowledge of her paintings, larger-than-life character, and heroic battle against physical disabilities filtered down to new generations. Thanks to the rise of the women's movement in the 1960s and 1970s, most people were more accepting of and in tune with professional, talented, and successful women. So Kahlo steadily gained not only fame but also a kind of mythical, cult-figure status. Her new identity became that of a gifted female artist who defied and ultimately defeated the forces of fate and a male-dominated society that had tried to keep her down.

Kahlo's memory and artistic reputation received two strong boosts in 1983. One was the publication of a major biography of her by respected art historian Hayden Herrera. A bestseller, the well-researched, moving book introduced Frida Kahlo to the much wider audience that exists outside of art circles. (Other biographies of Kahlo followed, but Herrera's remains the definitive one.) The other shot of adrenalin to Kahlo's reputation in 1983 took the form of a feature film—*Frida, Naturaleza Viva*—

A United States Postal Service stamp honoring Kahlo is revealed in 2001.

made in Mexico (and distributed in the United States as *Frida*). It was directed by Paul Leduc and starred popular Mexican actress Ofelia Medina in the title role.

From there, Frida Kahlo's image as an artist and a successful, eccentric, and courageous woman grew little by little each year. Artists of all kinds memorialized her in their works. In 1994, for example, American jazz flautist James Newton released an album titled *Suite for Frida Kahlo*.

In 2001, Kahlo's image appeared on a U.S. postage stamp, the first time in history that a Hispanic woman had been so honored. The following year, another feature film—the American-made *Frida*—was released worldwide. Directed by Julie Taymor, it starred Salma Hayek (who also coproduced the film) as Frida, Alfred Molina as Diego Rivera, Geoffrey Rush as Leon Trotsky, and Diego Luna as Alejandro Arias. The movie was nominated for six Oscars and won two. The year 2009 witnessed the publication of a major novel about Kahlo's life—*The Lacuna*, written by Barbara Kingsolver. Still another posthumous honor came in 2010 when the Bank of Mexico issued a new 500-peso bill with Rivera's image on the front and Kahlo's face, along with one of her paintings, on the back.

The Skyrocketing Value of Her Work

These and other similar tributes to Kahlo's memory and achievements made her internationally famous and thereby affected the way people viewed her paintings. Throughout the 1990s and beyond, her works appeared in major art exhibitions across the world. In February 2002, for instance, her paintings figured prominently in a special exhibition at Washington, DC's National Museum of Women in the Arts.

A much bigger commemoration of her work came in 2007, which marked the hundredth anniversary of her birth. The largest showing of her paintings ever held, it took place at Mexico's Palace of Fine Arts, where her body had laid in state in 1954. Included in the exhibit were paintings on loan from museums and individuals in San Francisco, Detroit, Miami, Minneapolis, Los Angeles, and elsewhere, as well as Mexico. In all, about a third of her roughly two hundred canvases had been gathered in one place. Also on display were several of her letters, some of which had never been seen by the public. After the show closed, a large portion of these paintings and letters toured major U.S. museums in the last months of 2007.

Another way that Kahlo's art was reevaluated during her gradual rise to global fame was the perceived monetary value of her paintings. During her lifetime she had sold only a few, and those had earned her at best only a few hundred dollars each. Most of the rest were given away to friends and relatives or remained part of her estate when she died.

This gross underappreciation of the value of her work began to change slightly more than two decades after her death. In

1977 the noted New York City auction house Sotheby's sold her painting *Tree of Hope* (1946) for $19,000. Two years later, her *Self-Portrait with Monkey* (1940) sold for $44,000.

Although these prices would have astounded and delighted Kahlo in her own day, they were swiftly eclipsed as her fame began to skyrocket in the 1980s and 1990s. For example, the same painting that sold for $44,000 in 1979 was purchased by the pop star Madonna for $1 million in the late 1980s. Similarly, the *Portrait of Cristina* (1928) was auctioned in 1988 for $198,000 and only a few years later sold again for $1,655,750. In 1995, Kahlo's *Self-Portrait with Monkey and Parrot* (1942) sold for $3,192,500; in 2000, *Self-Portrait, Time Flies* (1929) fetched a price of $5,065,750; and in 2006, *Roots* (1943) sold for $5,616,000.

An Example for Others

These phenomenal prices, along with critical raves from art critics, art historians, art dealers, and art collectors alike, have made Frida Kahlo one of the most admired painters in history. Also, experts agree that she eventually surpassed her husband to become the most famous and beloved of all Mexican painters. Yet fame and money were not the only important aspects of Kahlo's formidable legacy. Perhaps the greatest of all was the tremendous boost she gave to aspiring female artists. "I believe it is crucial," Judy Chicago writes,

> to examine Kahlo's legacy in relationship to the remarkable emergence of women artists in the second half of the twentieth century. For many centuries women artists were disadvantaged by a lack of training and professional opportunities along with assumptions about the proper role of women [in art]. As this began to change, the barriers began to fall, though not without a fight. . . . One reason why Frida Kahlo is so important is that, in addition to her artistic legacy, she signaled the moment when women artists began to

Opposite page: Portrait of Cristina, which was bought for more than $1.6 million in the early 1990s, is one of several Kahlo paintings that have sold for millions of dollars.

A MODEL OF A FABULOUS LIFE

Noted scholar and expert on Latin American art Victor Zamudio Taylor explains here why he and so many other art authorities think Frida Kahlo was a great painter.

Frida Kahlo is an artist who permits us to see the world in a different way. Frida Kahlo's works address very, very contradictory aspects of our culture. She deals with death, with love, with suffering, with history. She's constantly asking herself the following questions: Who am I? And what is my place in this world? And why am I here, what is my mission? What am I going to do with myself? How do I reconfigure myself and make myself who I want to be against all odds? I think that Frida Kahlo's importance in contemporary culture refers to two aspects: one, that our culture is very empty and hungry for meaning and seeking models of those who have led a fabulous life and who have . . . come to terms with very adverse conditions and made something for themselves, and also made their universe make sense. So we're attracted to Frida Kahlo as a kind of reflection of our own cultural condition. Across cultures and across time. But we're also attracted to Frida Kahlo because she's very powerful, and because she is a great artist. She's a source, an unstoppable fountain of thought-provoking ideas.

Interview with Victor Zamudio Taylor by Amy Stechler, 2005. *The Life and Times of Frida Kahlo*: PBS. www.pbs.org/weta/fridakahlo/today/taylor.html.

break the historic silence about women's experiences, thereby helping to lay the groundwork for an aesthetic [artistic] narrative of our own, one that is destined to redefine the history of art so that it includes the voices of many people rather than just a privileged few.[64]

A line of people winds outside of Mexico City's Palace of Fine Arts while waiting to see an exhibit of Kahlo's paintings in 2007. She is considered the most famous and beloved of all Mexican painters.

Herrera agrees and adds:

For women everywhere, and especially for women artists, Frida is an example of persevering strength. She painted against great odds. She worked in a macho culture and in the heyday of muralism, when a woman making small, highly personal easel paintings did not win much respect. She was not discouraged by the enormous fame and ferocious artistic drive of her husband.[65]

Finally, Kahlo left behind a legacy of optimism for those who, like she did, suffer from chronic pain, depression, sadness, and/or loneliness. She continued to turn out paintings no matter how much pain she was in, demonstrating that someone who is physically and/or emotionally disabled can still show strength, and work, and achieve, and inspire others. In an interview, Herrera said:

Frida's legacy . . . for people in general . . . has been this example of strength, and her story is a strength-giving story. . . . People come to me sometimes [when I'm giving] a Frida lecture somewhere, and . . . say that she's changed their lives because [they got] from her this idea that you can just keep struggling and keep working and deal with adversity and keep on going and come up with something that makes life, a whole life, seem worthwhile.[66]

Notes

Introduction: An Unquenchable Thirst for Life

1. Valmantas Budrys. "Neurological Deficits in the Life and Works of Frida Kahlo." *European Neurology* vol. 55, no. 1 (2006): p. 10.
2. Quoted in Hayden Herrera. *Frida Kahlo: The Paintings*. New York: Perennial, 2002, p. 218.
3. Quoted in "Art History Archive: Frida Kahlo." www.arthistoryarchive .com/arthistory/surrealism/Frida -Kahlo.html.
4. Quoted in Herrera. *Frida Kahlo: The Paintings*, p. 226.
5. Frida Kahlo. *The Diary of Frida Kahlo: An Intimate Self-Portrait*. New York: Harry N. Abrams, 2005, pp. 279–280.
6. Quoted in "Art History Archive: Frida Kahlo."
7. Salomon Grimberg. *Frida Kahlo*. North Dighton, MA: JG Press, 2002, p. 7.

Chapter 1: Her Childhood in the Blue House

8. Kahlo. *The Diary of Frida Kahlo*, p. 281.
9. Quoted in Hayden Herrera. *Frida: A Biography of Frida Kahlo*. New York: Harper and Row, 2002, p. 18.
10. Kahlo. *The Diary of Frida Kahlo*, p. 282.
11. Kahlo. *The Diary of Frida Kahlo*, p. 282.
12. Quoted in Herrera. *Frida*, p. 14.
13. Quoted in Herrera. *Frida*, p. 15.
14. Budrys. "Neurological Deficits"
15. Quoted in Jack Rummel. *Frida Kahlo: A Spiritual Biography*. New York: Crossroad, 2000, p. 28.
16. Herrera. *Frida*, p. 26.
17. Quoted in Herrera. *Frida*, p. 35.
18. Quoted in Rummel. *Frida Kahlo*, p. 52.
19. Quoted in Rummel. *Frida Kahlo*, pp. 52–53.
20. Quoted in Herrera. *Frida*, p. 49.
21. Quoted in Rummel. *Frida Kahlo*, p. 53.
22. Quoted in Bertram D. Wolfe. "Rise of Another Rivera." *Vogue*, November 1, 1938, p. 131.

Chapter 2: Her Two Loves: Art and Diego

23. Frida Kahlo. *The Letters of Frida Kahlo: Cartas Apasionadas* Compiled by Martha Zimora. San Francisco: Chronicle, 1995, p. 25.
24. Charles Moffat. "A Biography of Frida Kahlo." The Art History Archive: "Frida Kahlo." www.art

historyarchive.com/arthistory/surreal
ism/Frida-Kahlo.html.

25. Rummel. *Frida Kahlo*, p. 63.

26. Diego Rivera. *My Art, My Life: An Autobiography*. New York: Citadel, 1960, pp. 128–129.

27. Quoted in Herrera. *Frida*, p. 87.

28. Herrera. *Frida Kahlo: The Paintings*, pp. 55–57.

29. Quoted in Mike Brooks. "Complete Biography of Frida Kahlo." Frida Kahlo Fans. www.fridakahlofans .com/biocomplete.html.

30. Quoted in Brooks. "Complete Biography of Frida Kahlo."

31. Quoted in Rummel. *Frida Kahlo*, p. 75.

32. Mike Brooks. "Portrait of Lupe Marin." www.fridakahlofans.com /c0035.htm.

Chapter 3: Her Adventures in Gringolandia

33. Bertram D. Wolfe. *The Fabulous Life of Diego Rivera*. New York: Cooper Square Press, 2000, pp. 395–396.

34. Herrera. *Frida Kahlo: The Paintings*, pp. 61–62.

35. Rummel. *Frida Kahlo*, p. 88.

36. Mike Brooks. "Roots." Frida Kahlo Fans. www.fridakahlofans.com /c0420.html.

37. Herrera. *Frida*, p. 121.

38. Quoted in Herrera. *Frida*, pp. 135–136.

39. Mike Brooks. "Henry Ford Hospital (The Flying Bed)." Frida Kahlo Fans. www.fridakahlofans.com /c0090.html.

40. Rivera. *My Art, My Life*, p. 202.

41. Rummel. *Frida Kahlo*, p. 97.

42. Grimberg. *Frida Kahlo*, pp. 7–8.

43. Quoted in Judy Chicago. *Frida Kahlo: Face to Face*. New York: Prestel, 2010, p. 172.

Chapter 4: Her Growing Fame as an Artist

44. Quoted in Lisa W. Rogers. "Frida Kahlo: The Suicide of Dorothy Hale." http://lisawallerrogers .wordpress.com/2009/04/30/frida -kahlo-the-suicide-of-dorothy -hale.

45. Quoted in Herrera. *Frida*, p. 230.

46. Quoted in "Art History Archive: Frida Kahlo."

47. Moffat. "A Biography of Frida Kahlo."

48. Quoted in "Art History Archive: Frida Kahlo."

49. Quoted in Herrera. *Frida Kahlo: The Paintings*, pp. 135–136.

50. Chicago. *Frida Kahlo*, p. 91.

51. Mike Brooks. "The Wounded Table." www.fridakahlofans.com/c0354 .html.

52. Quoted in Chicago. *Frida Kahlo*, p. 148.

53. Quoted in Herrera. *Frida*, p. 298.

54. Kahlo. *The Diary of Frida Kahlo*, p. 213.

55. Grimberg. *Frida Kahlo*, p. 32.

56. Mike Brooks. "The Wounded Deer." Frida Kahlo Fans. www.fridakahlo fans.com/c0540.html.

57. Richard Dorment. "When the Artist Is the Canvas." *Telegraph*, June 8, 2005. www.telegraph.co.uk/culture /art/3643382/When-the-artist-is -the-canvas.html.

58. Quoted in "Art History Archive: Frida Kahlo."

59. Quoted in Herrera. *Frida,* pp. 407–409.
60. Quoted in "Art History Archive: Frida Kahlo."
61. Quoted in Herrera. *Frida*, p. 433.

Chapter 5: Her Legacy of Optimism

62. Quoted in Amy Stechler. "Understanding Frida Today." *The Life and Times of Frida Kahlo: PBS.* www .pbs.org/weta/fridakahlo/today /index.html.
63. Herrera. *Frida*, p. 439.
64. Chicago. *Frida Kahlo*, pp. 12, 15.
65. Herrera. *Frida Kahlo: The Paintings*, p. 224.
66. Interview with Hayden Herrera by Amy Stechler, 2005. *The Life and Times of Frida Kahlo: PBS.* www.pbs .org/weta/fridakahlo/today/herrera .html.

For More Information

Books

Judy Chicago. *Frida Kahlo: Face to Face*. New York: Prestel, 2010. Chicago, an artist of repute herself, teamed up with art historian Frances Borzello to produce this huge, insightful, nicely illustrated volume about Kahlo and her work.

Jacques and Natasha Gelman Collection. *Frida Kahlo, Diego Rivera, and Twentieth-Century Mexican Art*. Translated by Molly Stevens et al. New York: Distributed Art Publishers, 2000. This handsome catalog of art reproductions and commentary about Mexican artists was printed to accompany a major exhibition that toured the western United States in 2000.

Salomon Grimberg. *Frida Kahlo*. North Dighton, MA: JG Press, 2002. A beautifully mounted book with numerous, large, full-color plates of Kahlo's most famous works with short but informative accompanying text.

Hayden Herrera. *Frida: A Biography of Frida Kahlo*. New York: Harper and Row, 2002. The definitive modern biography of Kahlo, this book was the principal basis for the 2002 Miramax film about her life.

Hayden Herrera. *Frida Kahlo: The Paintings*. New York: Perennial, 2002. The companion volume to the above book, this one focuses on her paintings, with much useful commentary.

Frida Kahlo. *The Diary of Frida Kahlo: An Intimate Self-Portrait*. New York: Harry N. Abrams, 2005. Frida's diary is unusual because she illustrated it with numerous color drawings, which are faithfully reproduced in this printing.

Patrick Marnham. *Dreaming with His Eyes Open: A Life of Diego Rivera*. Berkeley: University of California Press, 2000. This is arguably the best documented and most thorough biography of Rivera (whose autobiography is riddled with inaccuracies). Marnham provides plenty of insights into the artist's stormy, passionate relationship with Frida Kahlo.

Carole Maso. *Beauty Is Convulsive: The Passion of Frida Kahlo*. Berkeley, CA: Counterpoint, 2002. The author has effectively interwoven various aspects of Kahlo's life into a series of verses that pay homage to the great Mexican artist.

John Morrison. *Frida Kahlo*. Philadelphia: Chelsea House, 2003. This excellent general introduction to Kahlo's life and artworks is aimed at high school and junior high school readers.

Jack Rummel. *Frida Kahlo: A Spiritual Biography*. New York: Crossroad, 2000. This is one of the more informative and well-written of the recent biographies of Kahlo.

Bertram D. Wolfe. *The Fabulous Life of Diego Rivera*. New York: Cooper Square Press, 2000. A thoroughly compelling biography of Kahlo's husband, with much information about her, their marriage, and their art.

Internet Sources

Charlie Rose.com. "Interview with Salma Hayek." (www.charlie rose.com/view/interview/2307). Commentator Charlie Rose interviews noted actress Salma Hayek about her portrayal of Frida Kahlo in the popular 2002 movie *Frida*.

Frida Kahlo Fans. "Biography of Frida Kahlo." (www.fridakahlofans.com /biocomplete.html). This brief biography of Kahlo is the work of a group of dedicated devotees of the artist who call themselves "Frida Kahlo Fans." They also provide links to a very useful gallery of Kahlo's paintings, arranged by year, a detailed chronology of her life, a long list of books about Kahlo, along with detailed reviews, and videos of home movies of Kahlo and Diego Rivera.

San Francisco Museum of Modern Art. "Diego Rivera's Art Manifesto." (www.sfmoma.org/explore/multi media/videos/49). This site contains a short video showing Rivera painting his murals while his voice can be heard delivering (in Spanish) his views on independence in art.

San Francisco Museum of Modern Art. "Frida in Love" (www.sfmoma .org/explore/multimedia/videos /132). This short but stunning video shows old films (in color) of Frida at home wearing her signature brightly-colored dresses and interacting with her husband Diego Rivera.

Websites

Frida Kahlo: The Complete Works (www.frida-kahlo-foundation.org). This site catalogs 101 of Kahlo's paintings and includes a brief biography.

Official website for Casa Azul (www .museofridakahlo.org.mx/servicio singles.html). This is the main page for the English version of the site for the Blue House museum. Click on the links provided to find valuable information on the house, Frida, and Diego Rivera.

Index

Credits

Picture Credits

Text Credits

Fifteen text excerpts from *Frida: A Biography of Frida Kahlo* by Hayden Herrera. Copyright © 1983 by Hayden Herrera. Reprinted by permission of HarperCollins Publishers.

About the Author

Historian Don Nardo is best known for his books for young people about the ancient and medieval worlds. These include volumes on the arts of ancient cultures, such as Mesopotamian arts and literature; Egyptian sculpture and monuments; Greek temples; Roman amphitheaters; medieval castles; general histories of sculpture, painting, and architecture through the ages; and biographies of renowned artists. Mr. Nardo lives with his wife, Christine, in Massachusetts.